SIDETRACKED TO SURRENDER

A True Story of Overcoming Trials and Finding Redemption

in God's Love

DONNA BESS

PUBLISHING
NASHVILLE, TENNESSEE

Sidetracked to Surrender: A true story of overcoming trials and finding redemption in God's love, ©2024 Donna Bess

Paperback ISBN: 978-1-953211-43-9; eBook ISBN: 978-1-953211-44-6
Hardback ISBN: 978-1-953211-45-3; Audio book ISBN: 978-1-953211-46-0
Editor: Loral Pepoon, cowriterpro.com
Publisher: Selah Press Publishing

Scripture references marked NIV are from https://www.biblegateway.com/ Holy Bible, New International Version®, NIV® Copyright ©1973, 1978, 1984, 2011 by Biblica, Inc.® Used by permission. All rights reserved worldwide. Scripture references marked MSG https://www.biblegateway.com/ The Message (MSG) Copyright © 1993, 2002, 2018 by Eugene H. Peterson.Scripture references marked NLT https://www.biblegateway.com/ New Living Translation (NLT) *Holy Bible*, New Living Translation, copyright © 1996, 2004, 2015 by Tyndale House Foundation. Used by permission of Tyndale House Publishers, Inc., Carol Stream, Illinois 60188. All rights reserved. Scripture references marked TLB https://www.biblegateway.com/ Living Bible (TLB) The Living Bible copyright © 1971 by Tyndale House Foundation. Used with permission of Tyndale House Publishers Inc., Carol Stream, Illinois 60188. All rights reserved. Scripture references marked ESV https://www.biblegateway.com/ English Standard Version (ESV) The Holy Bible, English Standard Version. ESV® Text Edition: 2016. Copyright © 2001 by Crossway Bibles, a publishing ministry of Good News Publishers.Scripture references marked NKJV https://www.biblegateway.com/New King James Version (NKJV) New King James Version®. Copyright © 1982 by Thomas Nelson. Used with permission. All rights reserved. Scripture references marked NASB https://www.biblegateway.com/New American Standard Bible (NASB) New American Standard Bible®, Copyright © 1960, 1971, 1977, 1995, 2020 by The Lockman Foundation. All rights reserved. Scripture references marked AMP https://www.biblegateway.com/Amplified Bible (**AMP**) Amplified Bible, Copyright © 2015 by The Lockman Foundation, La Habra, CA 90631. All rights reserved. Scripture references marked TPT https://www.bible.com/bible The Passion Translation® is a registered trademark of Passion & Fire Ministries, Inc. Copyright © 2020 Passion & Fire Ministries, Inc.

Editorial liberties: Names of God and references to Him are capitalized, and satan and the enemy are lowercased.

Disclaimer: The conversations in this book all come from the author's recollections. They are not written to represent word-for-word transcripts. Rather the author has re-told them in a way that evokes the feeling and meaning of what was said. In all instances, the essence of the dialogue is a close and accurate account of what took place. The author has changed the names of several individuals and places and may have changed some identifying characteristics and details for the protection of many in this book.

ENDORSEMENTS

The book, *Sidetracked to Surrender*, by Donna Bess, is a powerful page-turner that is hard to put down. One moment I had tears streaming down my face; the next moment I was laughing and in complete awe at what God had done. Donna writes her story in such a relatable, authentic, and compelling way that you're drawn into every scene as if you were in the room with her. You can't wait to see what happens next. You can feel the rawness of emotion on every page.

This is a book that touches your heart and leaves you a more compassionate person. It is full of the goodness of God in the hardest times, and it brings goosebumps of joy in the redemptive times. I would definitely recommend this book to anyone who is going through a tough season. It will encourage, strengthen, and renew your hope that when you surrender to a loving God, He will never forsake you.

Missy Maxwell Worton
Award-Winning Author, Founder of the Warrior Writers

Seldom has a story so captured my heart as from the new book, *Sidetracked to Surrender*, by author Donna Bess.

When you read a book and keep remembering the story days later, you realize you've experienced a great storyteller, whose powerful and insightful words brings you emotionally right into each event. I will remember this overcoming testimony for a long time.

God writes beautiful stories, and He has enabled Donna to share her difficult but redemptive and beautiful discovery of His love and grace. As you read, you too will be given a new understanding of the pain of life but also the wonderful assurance of how God is at work in every death, loss, and circumstance.

Pastor Jerry Bryant
Worship City Alliance, Nashville, Tennessee

You will not want to put this book down as you move through chapter after chapter of a life that is rich because of a great love that only comes from a passionate relationship with Jesus. This is a frank discussion of personal pain and joy and the faithfulness of God. Even when Donna turns her back on Jesus, she discovers His love even more deeply than ever.

Whether you are a new believer or have followed Jesus for years, this book is loaded with lessons of a surrendered life. Get a cup of coffee, get ready to dig in, and be encouraged!

Marion Farrar

Tennessee General, Reformation Prayer Network

Founder, Nashville Women's Conference

Dedication

First, my dedication must go to my Beloved, faithful friend, and Lord. You held me while I wept in shame and fear. My disappointment that I was not a better Christian, You revealed to me, was not Your heart at all. Broken by traumas, tragedies, and poor decisions, I felt I might never be free again, yet You broke the chains off my soul and taught me to forgive, love, and trust again. I want to honor You, Lord, with our story of how You loved me back from despair to see Your truth and hope. It is a testimony to Your kindness that has led me to live again. I am grateful for Your grace, my Father, my Daddy.

Secondly, I wish to dedicate this book to my children, Mindy, Jarred, and Jenna. I continually marvel at your faith walk and how you each decided a long time ago that no matter what, you will follow Jesus. I am more grateful than words can express. I love your hearts for others and your tenacity to raise my grandchildren to honor our Lord with their lives. I am one blessed mom and nana.

With all my heart!

Why Did I Write This Book?

One morning, as I prayed, a question stirred in my heart: *Why?*

Why did I write this book?

Why did I lay bare my brokenness, exposing the messy and fragile parts of my life to you, my readers?

The answer came swiftly and powerfully: ***Because I have an audacious hope in the Lord, and I want you to have it, too!***

Paul writes in 1 Thessalonians 4:13 (NLT):"And now, dear brothers and sisters, we want you to know what will happen to the believers who have died so you will not grieve like people who have no hope."

This hope is not just a concept—it's a lifeline.

As you follow my journey through the pages of this book, through stories of extreme life situations that could have derailed destiny, you'll see the fight it sometimes took to hold on to hope. There were moments—many of them—where it felt like a battle just to keep my faith.

BUT GOD!

To you, my dear reader, I pray this truth will echo in your heart: No matter what you face, **He is faithful.**

In some of my darkest moments, I clung to a declaration—a mantra, if you will—that anchored me when everything around me seemed to crumble. It might be exactly what you need today.

Declare it boldly:

"It doesn't matter what I see or don't see.

It doesn't matter what I think or don't think.

It doesn't matter what I feel or don't feel.

I will trust Him."

Let this declaration be the heartbeat of your journey, as it has been for mine. Dare to hope, to trust, and to believe that the God who has carried me will carry you, too.

Chapter One
DIZZY

Being an adult means learning to survive in the
uncertainties of life in healthy ways
—Donna Bess

Farrell's Ice Cream Parlour in Altamonte, Florida, was a sweet sensation with a magical appeal to delight everyone and a surefire cure for the blues. With décor from the early 1900s with old-time red and white striped period costumes and straw boater hats, everyone was saturated with laughter, cacophonous piano music, and happy families enjoying their favorite flavors. Judy and I often went there in high school to manage our life difficulties and drown our sorrows in a sea of ice cream. But one day, we were there for a different reason. The day we thought was so far away for the seven years it had been since we have been each other's sidekick was only a blink of an eye. I remember our conversation like it was yesterday.

"Can you believe we are FINALLY high school graduates class of 1977?" I said with joy exuding from every syllable.

Judy, beaming from ear to ear, nodded, "I knooooowww." Judy, excitingly drawing out the word to punctuate the freedom of that statement, raised her hand to indicate it was time for a high five. Our hands met across from each other in the booth as she hollered, "We did it, and now our lives are our own to live as we please."

I responded, "Well, maybe in three-and-a half months, when we turn eighteen, it will be our own. But for now, we have the summer to enjoy our freedom from school, working to save money so we can move out ASAP, along with, of course, beach trips and a 'little' shopping, with emphasis on little!" We laughed in synchronous joy, with the understanding that much money would be needed for us to move into an apartment as soon as we celebrated our birthdays.

A waiter who was a gorgeous boy-next-door type of guy with sandy hair and bronze skin appeared. "You're new here, Dave," I said, noting his name tag. His smile revealed a perfect smile of gleaming white teeth.

"Yeah, I started last week. I guess you guys are regulars if you know that."

We both laughed, and I replied, "You can say that; who doesn't like a lot of noisy laughter and ice cream?"

He chuckled with a cheeky grin and a glint in his eye as he looked at Judy, "We have yummy sandwiches too."

Noting his flirty look at Judy who paid him no mind, I laughed at his attempt to upsell our check. "We have eaten them a few times, and what we had was good, but let's face it, there is a reason this place is known—for its ice cream!" He laughed, again beaming at Judy, and asked what he could get for us.

Dave was the type of boy that appealed to me, but Judy was not smitten. She was drawn to the bad boy—heavy metal, rough talking, far from the boy next-door. Dave was kind and therefore his flirtations fell completely flat for Judy, but they made me laugh. Judy, still beaming with the freedom she felt as we had officially moved from being high school students into adulthood, was feeling adventurous. "We each should order the 'Trough' and see if we could eat it," she said.

I raised my eyebrows to indicate the ridiculousness of that statement. Ferrell's signature sundae was called the Pig's Trough and contained a double banana split with six large scoops of ice cream and all the toppings. The singing, dancing, and joking servers enticed the customers to gorge on the mountainous contents. Sirens rang with raucous cheers if you managed to consume it all. Looking at Judy like she was allowing the joy of graduation to cause all sense to leave her mind, I said, "Judy, you and I both will not be able to finish one, let alone each of us finishing one by ourselves!"

She laughed, "You are probably right, but let's try." Judy was 4'11" and petite with a tiny appetite to match. I, on the other hand, was 5'6", with an additional thirty-five pounds on her. I knew which of us was more likely to eat three days' worth of calories in a single setting, and it wasn't Judy!

Denying her my participation, I said, "You go ahead, and I will cheer you on!" She laughed at my admission that though I could probably do it, I wasn't willing to risk the profound stomachache that would likely result. Having a parade of servers singing, sirens ringing, and wild applause for the well-won battle of gluttony was not worth it to me. No thank you!

Dave left with our normal order, and we laughed at the ridiculous consideration and the acknowledgment that neither of us needed to risk the effects of such a conquest.

Judy had been my saving grace since our last year of elementary school, and we always counted it providential that we met. In our minds, the circumstances of our miracle meeting meant we were destined to be friends forever. Born two days apart and ten miles away from each other in New Jersey, but not meeting until sixth grade in Florida, surely pointed to something greater than coincidence. We believed it was fate that we would always be around each other, especially when I found out my parents originally planned to name me Judy until my mom discovered that my dad had an old girlfriend with that same name. Not surprisingly, my name was changed.

Judy was the oldest of three children in her family; I was the youngest of three children in mine. We were straddled in life with only brothers, so we became the sisters we wanted and needed. She spent almost as much time in my room as in her own room. Judy was by my side for dinner, vacation, every weekend, and many times in between. As young teens, we rode our bikes to Kmart to shop for matching clothes. Despite our differing body shapes and sizes, we managed to secure enough matching outfits to become known as the "twins" to our friends at school.

Like our sizes, our personalities were very different. Judy was quiet and pensive, and I was loud and boisterous. I often laughed loudly, annoying some, but she never minded that about me. And even though she would hide behind me when I laughed, she politely defended me when others complained. Our differences make me laugh even today, decades later.

With neither of our families remotely interested in attending church, Judy and I spent Sunday mornings with Casey Kasem's American Top 40. From 9 a.m. to noon, we sat on the floor in my room, writing down each song and the artist on a piece of paper with the help of a speaker-turned-writing table. It was a special hangout time that lasted all through high school.

I couldn't understand why the girl who could be popular by anyone's standards chose to be friends with me—and me alone. Even when she became a cheerleader in eighth grade, she only associated with the squad members when required. Otherwise, we were always together throughout junior high. As the "tiny one," she needed a base to practice her cheers, which I was happy to assist her with. I had been taking tap, ballet, jazz, and acrobatics for six years. I prided myself on my not-so-stellar cheerleading skills, which is why I never chose to participate officially in that activity. But Judy overlooked what I thought were inadequacies and made me feel included by teaching me every cheer. I was then ready to attend every game and cheer from the stands as part of the pep squad.

We started playing tennis most weekends at the high school, which was a short bike ride away from both of our homes. We knew the point was to hit the ball back and forth, but other than that, we didn't have much skill at that particular sport. Our lack of knowledge never stopped us from our commitment to spend about two hours each weekend perfecting our volley of the ball. Junior high was amazing. By the end of junior high, we slowly departed from our "twin" identity as our likes and dislikes naturally changed. Though our personalities were changing as well, our relationship was unhindered.

Surprisingly, high school was even better than I could have imagined! As we received more freedom, we would leave on our bikes in the morning and be gone much of the day. We rode around for hours, only stopping for lunch and bathroom breaks at one of our homes, and then back to the road we went. About once a month, we used our allowance money to take the city bus to the mall. After we were done shopping, we visited our favorite German restaurant, where we could sit at the bar and eat our turkey sandwich with chips and feel so grown up. This once-a-month outing was always much anticipated and incredibly enjoyed.

As we matured, our relationship entered greater depths. I began to understand who Judy was and why she was so comfortable with only me as her close friend. This revelation was sharpened in the eleventh grade when we both were given cars for our sixteenth birthday. Judy's dad, whom she rarely saw and hardly mentioned, bought her an older model green Gremlin. She took pride in that car but somehow felt a little resentment that he seemed to think buying her a car would make up for his absenteeism as a father.

Hearing about how her dad treated her helped me understand how difficult it must have been to grow up in a broken home. Her situation also helped me develop gratitude for my family because I had two parents that loved me. My situation at home was far from perfect, but it was where Judy and I preferred to spend most of our time. I received my gold Nova hatchback a few weeks after Judy received her car. Our expression was, "Have wheels, will travel." And travel we did, with great enthusiasm!

Another shocking revelation about Judy's demeanor came one morning when I picked her up to go to the beach. Packed for a full day of fun in the sun, I pulled into her drive and honked the horn. She came out the door in our matching bikini and a long shirt as a cover up, but her face looked haunted and angry, not matching the excitement I knew we had for this glorious day. Following her with my questioning eyes, I searched for a clue as to the dark mood surrounding her. She walked quickly down the drive, jumped in my car, and said, "Go!" As if I was her getaway driver from some hostile situation.

I quickly backed out of the driveway and asked what was wrong.

She glared at her mother, who was mowing the front lawn. "Her," she growled.

I glanced and waved as her mom looked our way. "What happened?" I asked.

Hot tears streaming from her eyes, she asked, "Why does she need to dress like a teenager?" Her mom was mowing the lawn in a bikini. She was not fat, nor was she thin. Still not understanding, Judy said, "If I get some clothing she likes, she wants something similar, and I hate it. It embarrasses me."

Not fully understanding, I replied, "I'm sorry." Unsure how to address what seemed like a great offense, I changed the subject—a skill I had mastered over time to deal with her random but not completely infrequent sadness.

Judy's mom also liked to be in the crowd when Judy's cheerleading friends came over, which was probably why Judy stopped inviting them over in ninth grade. Whatever the case, my heart went out to her, and I understood why Judy was more comfortable in my home. We spent the night at her home only a handful of times. My parents embraced Judy as part of our family. I was never told no when I asked if she could come over.

Shortly after our sixteenth birthdays, both Judy and I were hired at Disney World. We worked the same schedule in the same location. Our last two years of high school were filled with togetherness to and from work, beach trips, mall trips, and making sweet memories.

Neither of us had the support of our parents to go to college, and we knew working for a few years to get some money would be necessary. My father declared emphatically, "I will not pay for you to go to college to get married and have babies." Her parents were not interested in helping her, stating that she needed to make her own way.

However, with hopes and dreams of a brighter tomorrow, our ambition was not stifled. Judy and I graduated from high school with different paths in mind. Judy longed to be a journalist and travel the globe. She sought independence from her family as her life of hurt became increasingly evident. As for me, I didn't want to wander far from my father. I desired to attend a local college and become a teacher.

Our more independent personalities began shining brighter as time moved on. Summer still included mall trips and beach trips, even though our clothing styles were now markedly different. Mine was more ultra-feminine with satin, lace, and ruffled pastels. Judy's look was more heavy metal and dark. She wore t-shirts with the faces of the bandmembers from Kiss with their tongues hanging out.

On September 2, just twenty days before her eighteenth birthday and twenty-two days before mine, we headed to a Winter Park salon to get our hair done. Winter Park is an upscale area with boutiques and specialty shops lining the downtown streets about fifteen miles north of our Orlando-area homes. We intended to follow our salon appointment with some window gazing and lunch. However, rain and unseasonably cooler weather put a damper on those plans. Deciding to skip lunch and shopping, we headed to Disney World, about thirty miles south of where we lived to get our paychecks instead.

We cruised down the interstate with my car radio serenading us with ABBA, Barry White, Donna Summer, and the like. Although Judy liked to listen to Kiss and other heavy metal/rock music, we only heard that when she drove. We learned to enjoy our differences, which brought humor to the relationship. The dreariness of the weather didn't match the joy we had in the car. As we drove, the weather changed to a sprinkling of rain, and the sun began to peak through the clouds like it did every afternoon in Orlando.

Suddenly, coming around a bend in the highway, we were met with a surprise—one that would change my life forever. The traffic was at a standstill, and the line of cars was too close for me to stop safely. My dad's lessons about defensive driving immediately came to mind:

"Never slam on brakes on a wet road. Pump them in quick bursts." My foot was pumping madly on the brake, and my eyes were wide with adrenaline now slamming my heart into my chest. Judy screamed, "Donna!" with a terror that could not compete with adrenaline pulsating through me. With the median to my left, I quickly assessed where to put my car and contemplated each action in some weird slow motion, the kind only seen in movies.

First, I pumped my way to the wide median, as it seemed long enough for me to stop, but then wet grass declared otherwise. As I approached an area surrounded by guardrails, reason led me to see that turning the car around was the only option. Otherwise, I would plow through the railing into the open space that leads to the highway running beneath the opening. Turning wide right then sharp left to get the car to comply towards the other direction was working. As I made the U-turn, I thought we were in the clear. However, before I could breathe a sigh of relief, my right rear tire hydroplaned into oncoming traffic. Suddenly, the crunching sound of metal at the right rear bumper sent my car in a counterclockwise spin. Before we stopped spinning, a second hit from the front driver's side sent the vehicle backward a few feet and then a spin clockwise. Judy screamed my name again, and something hit my lap. A third hit and crushing of metal in the rear lurched my car forward. Then another spin happened, and the car finally stopped, facing the same direction I originally intended.

Silence.

Chapter Two
DERAILING THE FUTURE

Trials and sorrows mark us like an indelible ink,
forever shaping who we become.
—Donna Bess

Shaking my head to stop the spinning motion in my brain, I saw Judy's head lying in my lap. As I looked, I saw her eyes roll back and then close. "Judy," I screamed as I shook her. No response! A louder, more desperate tone with a harder shake, as if trying to jar her from a deep sleep, "Judy!" No response. Panic rose again in my chest, and my stomach tumbled like a tennis shoe in the dryer. I lifted her head off my lap and jumped from the car. Racing to the passenger's side, I opened the door. "Judy?" I yelled. Recognizing she would not wake up; I stood trying to figure out what to do next. Traffic was stopped in both directions on the busiest interstate through Orlando, and every pair of eyes from a hundred cars were now focused on us—actually on me!

I looked up to see a man standing in the median taking pictures. I was incensed and yelled, "What are you doing? Stop taking pictures and get help!" Feeling helpless, I squatted beside the open passenger door and put my hand on Judy's leg. Whimpering, barely above a whisper, I pleaded, "Help! Please, somebody help!"

Fear and panic now caused my body to shake uncontrollably. The loud silence in those moments bounced around in my head. Tears began to fall. What happened? Just moments ago, we were laughing and making plans to sneak in one more beach trip before the weather turned too cool. Now? My brain was frozen in time. "Judy, please wake up," I cried. Though I had never prayed before, I started now with a plea for this unknown God to intervene. Less of a whimper and more of an agonizing petition for this God to insert Himself here, at this moment, and "Help her, please!"

As if in direct response to my appeal, I heard sirens and a fire truck, ambulance, and paramedic truck arrived all at one time. Traffic was stopped in both directions, and I didn't know how they managed to get to the accident scene so quickly. But they had arrived, and I was so relieved. My mind again petitioned the unknown person that others pray to, *Please, make everything okay!*

First responders piled out of their vehicles and headed toward us. A fireman came first to me and asked if I was hurt. My attention was on him, but I heard a man's voice behind me in the car talking to someone. He said, "Not responsive." Just as I was about to turn to look at who was speaking, the fireman urged me forward with his hand on my elbow, encouraging me to follow him away from the car. I obeyed without a thought, like a child being led.

He led me to the emergency command truck on the opposite side of the median and told me to sit. He put a blanket around me. He asked again, "Miss, are you okay?"

Another fireman came over and said to him, "Her name is Donna."

He asked again, "Donna, do you have any pain?" I could hear, but my brain could not engage to form words. All I could do was stare across the median to where Judy lay. With a gentle shake of my shoulder and a more commanding voice, he said again, "Donna?"

As if broken from a trance, I locked eyes with him and said, "I'm okay. Can I see Judy?"

He was quick with the response. "Let them take care of her, and let's see about you. Do you have any pain?"

Pain, I thought? *Do I have any pain? Think Donna. Does anything hurt?* I looked down to the only pain I could locate—a small red mark on my left shin where my stockings now had a run. "Only a little right here," I pointed down.

He said, "Yeah, that is probably from hitting the emergency brake with your shin in the accident. Do you have any other pain?"

I replied, "No. Can I see Judy now?"

As if providential, one of the men surrounding Judy stood and said, "She can come over now." Finally, I thought. Though probably only a minute or two, it seemed like half an hour.

But before we made it over, three men rose and said in unison, "Take her back. She will have to see her at the hospital." In a few moments, Judy was loaded into the back of an ambulance. With lights and sirens, she was gone from my sight. The sound of the siren grew more distant, and my heart grew more anxious.

Weakened by the adrenaline flooding my body, the fireman assisted me with stepping into the front seat of the large truck, ensuring my seatbelt was secure before taking his place in the driver's seat. We headed to the hospital in deafening silence. Consuming fear, a wicked headache, and nausea tormented my resolve to stay calm. The whirring sound of the siren on the ambulance, though too far to hear now, was still echoing in my mind. Within ten to fifteen minutes, we pulled into the ambulance entrance of the hospital, and he again helped me from the truck.

He ushered me inside, directing me with his hand on my back and pointing ahead to where I needed to go in the overly crowded emergency room waiting area. Anxious and breathing harder, I reprimanded myself to calm down. This nightmare would be over soon. The fireman's calm and reassuring voice was guiding me, assuring me that I was not alone.

This large room with rows of chairs was wall-to-wall with people. Children were running around like it was some kind of playground. Loud, confusing noises and awful smells overwhelmed my senses as we walked to the "Triage" area. The fireman told the nurse I was in an accident, and my friend was brought here. She asked if I needed to be seen, and the fireman responded, "She was checked, and she is fine." "Donna, tell her your friend's name." I gave her Judy's name, but a quick search showed nobody was there by that name.

Confusion and panic quickened my breathing again. "Where is Judy? Did they take her someplace else?" The fireman told me to have a seat, and he would find out what happened. After ushering me to a chair, he stepped away to talk on his radio but never took his eyes off me. After a moment, he came back and told me they were checking in to where Judy might be.

"Donna, come over here and contact your family," he said gently, trying to keep me calm. I returned to the triage area, and the nurse dialed my home number. My mom answered, and suddenly I had no voice.

I whispered, "Mom," my voice broke, and quivering sobs ensued. The fireman took over the call. Though probably unlikely, all eyes in the waiting room seemed to be on me. Perhaps the fireman drew their attention, but it made me want to run. But where?

The fireman finished the call and quietly said, "Your mom is on her way."

Agitated and stomach churning, I began to pace the hall where the fireman could still see me. We had been here long enough, and I still had no word on Judy. My thoughts were racing...*Is she at a different hospital? Did she wake up, and they discovered she was okay, and they didn't even bring her in? Why was I not being told anything?* The smells in this waiting room engulfed me, and hysteria was just below the surface. My determination to remain strong was weakening; I was afraid and alone.

My legs again feeling weak, I retook my seat. *How much time has passed?* I couldn't tell, but it felt like well over an hour. *How come they won't let me see Judy?* Willing myself to calm down so I didn't vomit, this overcrowded sea of humanity smelled horribly. I looked up as I heard the sound of my mom's voice.

Mom was born and raised in Savannah, Georgia. She was more serious at home, but she would laugh occasionally at my dad's wisecracks. I sometimes felt a deep pain in my mom that I did not understand. When mom was with her four sisters, she was altogether different. She was loud, belly laughed to tears often, and rested in her band of sisterhood. I never considered my mom affectionate, but I knew she loved me as well as she knew how to love.

At that moment, she was a gift to my weary soul. I stood and embraced her with my face buried in her shoulder, allowing a release of pent-up fear to stream out as she held me. She didn't ask any questions of me or the fireman standing close by. I was so glad the fireman stayed with me and watched over me, but I was immensely grateful my mom had arrived to be by my side, even though I was not in the mood to talk.

A young woman sitting on the other side of my mom, probably in her early twenties, struck up a conversation with mom, telling my mom about her experience in this chaotic emergency room. When this girl had arrived, the emergency room staff associated her with a different victim, and they took her to identify her sister's body, but it wasn't her sister at all. The poor girl was so upset that she had to experience that nightmare. My mom sympathized, but she was rather quiet about this traumatic experience.

Mom turned back toward me and commented that traffic had been stopped in both directions, and that was why she hadn't gotten through sooner. She flagged down an officer and told him her daughter was in that wreck, and said she was trying to get to the hospital. He escorted her with flashing lights on the shoulder to the exit for the hospital.

With no energy to think about the accident scene, I couldn't say anything to my mom. I focused my attention straight ahead. The noise, the smells of antiseptic's failed attempt to cover something more putrid, and the tension of the unknown were taking its toll on me. Anxiety was causing a quake in my body, and I felt weak as a lamb. *Why were they taking so long? They know something by now. My mom was trying to stay calm; I sensed she knew something but wasn't saying it to me. Did she see something? Did the fireman tell her something? Was she mad at me? Did she already tell Dad? Was he mad at me?*

At that time, a man dressed in scrubs came and asked for me. My mom stood and said, "Here she is." He told us to follow him, and we walked through the doors to a sterile, white-tiled hall with white walls. The sound of my shoes caused a repeated tapping noise that echoed irritatingly as we neared a door labeled "Counseling Room."

My brain was screaming, *Counseling Room? Where is Judy?*

The gentleman said, "The doctor will be here in just a moment." We took a seat in the tiny room that fit about eight people. Panic rose as I sat in this plain room with a few vases of fake flowers and several boxes of tissue placed strategically around. The setting gave an ominous feeling. In less than a minute, the doctor arrived beside Judy's mom, Cindy. The doctor's face was as neutral as a stiff portrait, but not Judy's mom. Her eyes and face were swollen and red. As she entered the room, she looked past me to my mother's eyes and said three words I could never have imagined. Her three words cut my soul, sidetracked my dreams and altered my life forever. With her face twisted in a haunted emotion that made me shiver with fear, she said dryly, "Judy is dead."

Chapter Three

CHOICES

Trauma shackles you to the scene of the crisis.
—Donna Bess

"NOOOOO" I yelled hysterically. A confused wail came from my core as I screamed, "It can't be possible," as if my emotions would make them re-evaluate their conclusions. "It can't be true. We didn't get hurt in the car. She can't be dead. Her side of the car didn't even get hit." Each reason elevated my hysteria until I saw that nobody in the room was responding. Instead, they were silent, staring at my meltdown with pity and completely unmoved by my convictions. My knees were weak, and I felt as if I might pass out. My mind went blank as a large piece of my heart died.

Sitting in the front passenger seat of my mom's car, my mind began to form thoughts again, and with that, adrenaline spiked, and racing thoughts returned as we made the painful drive home. The quiet in the car was a clear indication that each of us was in shock. Dreadful thoughts filled my mind in the silent drive. *I killed Judy. My dad will hate me forever. How can this be happening?* I thought about the accident and played each second repeatedly in my mind trying to find the cause of her death. *I ran my stockings, and Judy was dead. That isn't even possible. She didn't get tossed around; she didn't hit the window. Wait, did it happen, and I didn't notice? Could she have? Why can't I remember? There must be a mistake. Why would they not let me see her? How can she be dead? Did a car hit her? Think Donna! Dad will want an explanation!*

I was closer to home but no closer to answers; the cold sweat of trepidation filled my face. Fear of the consequences made me wish I had been the one who died. My dad will be angry and disappointed with me. Imagining his face moved me to fresh tears. I was so afraid. What could I say? *I wasn't speeding, but would he believe me? Doubtful, but that would be my fault because I often did, and he knew it. This must be all my fault. I have lost Judy, my best friend, and now, I will lose my dad too. He will never forgive me.*

Realizing my life and dreams were being sidetracked by the greatest tragedy I could have imagined filled me with the crushing weight of despair. Rehearsing in my mind, repeatedly, every movement, every word of our conversation, the weather, the music, and the surroundings, just looking for a cause, I could only conclude there was none, at least not one that made sense to me. Just then, the car jarring over the curb pulled me from my thoughts. I was home. My heart quickened, once again fearing what would happen when I walked through that door. Standing up to get out of the car felt nearly impossible. The heaviness of my soul and hours of adrenaline pulsing through my veins made me weak. Slowly we walked toward the front door with Mom in step behind me; I willed my legs to move forward. I opened the door, and Dad was standing there just inside the door.

Dad was a stocky 5'10" with giant arms of strength, retired Marine Corps drill sergeant beast of a man. He retired at a higher rank than a sergeant, but my thoughts growing up were that once a drill sergeant, always a drill sergeant. If my mom was not overly affectionate, my dad was less. He hugged me occasionally, and I knew he loved me. He never hit me, but I was terrified of disappointing him. I had seen encounters with my brothers that had left a lasting impression.

His face held questions. *Was he confused about why mom wasn't at home cooking dinner? Did he wonder where we had gone?* Though he did not speak, his face asked the obvious question—*What happened?* Mom quickly responded, "Donna was in a car accident, and Judy is dead," with a strong declaration of truth that deepened the pain.

As I steeled myself for his wrath, he moved toward me, and with the most unexpected movement, he embraced me. He pulled me close with the arms of a desperate man, and I inhaled deeply the tenderness of his hold. With tears in his eyes and a raspy passionate voice I had never heard before or since, he said, "I'm so glad you are all right." I clung to him in that moment of unanticipated mercy as tears of relief washed over me. I could hear his sniffle. *Wow, maybe he does care more about me than what I had done. He squeezed me tight. He didn't yell. He didn't express anger. He just enfolded me in his arms. No questions about Judy, what happened, or what my part was.* Just a hug and a simple statement packed with emotions I had not known from my father. Bewildered yet lifted by the moment, I didn't want to leave.

After moments in his arms, I slipped from his hold to retreat to my room. Alone, on my bed in the fetal position, with my pillow pressed to my face to stifle the sound of my guttural wail, my soul was releasing some of the terror that had been pummeling me since I came around the curve and saw the stopped traffic. Night had fallen before my heart stopped ricocheting around my chest. Unfortunately, the temporal throbbing in my head took up where my heart left off with an unbelievable pounding. I was lying there staring into the darkness. My life and future lie in waste. Because my relationship with my parents had grown more distant in the previous year, now, when I needed them most, the breach was too far to cross. I was alone and afraid. I needed Judy. The loneliness was crushing.

The next morning, I awoke with swollen eyes, a headache, a broken heart, hopelessness, and despair. I lay staring at the ceiling that had played out nightmares all night. I accepted the truth. Judy was gone, and there was a hole in my heart. I could feel myself sinking. I didn't know what to do next, but I couldn't just lie here. I had been trained to pull myself up by my bootstraps. What could I do? I have to move, or I will be swallowed in these shadows. Where should I go? Then it struck me—my only choice was to go to work.

I got dressed and went to the kitchen to make some toast. Mom and Dad sitting at the table with coffee and a newspaper, looked up at me. It was just like any other day and yet not like any other day. I could see the weight of life in their eyes, and I knew I was responsible. I mumbled with my mouth full to hide the truth that I was far from okay, "I'm going to work."

Mom asked if I was okay, and I nodded yes. She said surprisedly, "You know, you don't have to go to work."

I thought, *So I stay home and wallow in the silent grave I have created in this house. No thanks!* Explaining that I needed to get Judy's things out of her locker seemed to satisfy her questions. My dad was quiet. That was not unusual because he often was, but today I needed something. I didn't have a clue what, but whatever it was, it wasn't there.

As I was driving my mom's car the twenty-four miles to work, every song on the radio brought tears. Hitting the off button on the dash to stop the flood of reminders, I opted for silence. Now with only the company of my dark thoughts, I wondered how I would make it. The last eight miles were filled with curves, and on the first sharp curve, my purse slid across the seat, hitting my leg, and a flashback to Judy's head in my lap was fresh as if it was just a breath ago. Fear and panic incapacitated me. Violent shaking and heaving sobs forced me to the side of the road. With my head still buried against my arms that are folded on the steering wheel, Linda, a friend from high school and an employee at Disney walked up to my car and tapped on my window. Beside Linda was her father. They were on their way to work, and they saw me on the side of the road and stopped to see if they could help. Her eyes filled with tears at the sight of me; she knew. Everyone knew.

I could tell by their careful wording that they knew all the details of what happened. The major interstate in Orlando being shut down with traffic for two hours in both directions made for significant news coverage. Linda sat in the passenger seat of my car, and her father leaned on the door frame. She asked, "What can we do?"

Suddenly realizing I would probably be asked that question a million times, I just shook my head. "Nothing." Lost in thought again, *What can anyone do? Nothing will bring Judy back, so...that question has no answer.* Clearing my throat and blowing my nose, I assured her I was fine and thanked them for stopping. Linda offered to drive my car the rest of the way, and her dad would follow. "No, thank you," I said, responding quickly. I didn't want to talk, and I was afraid of the questions.

Their kindness helped me calm down. I assured them I was okay, but they followed me the rest of the way to work. I parked, and they rode the shuttle from the parking lot to the tunnels under Disney with me. I could feel their eyes on me, but they said nothing else. I had a feeling that people staring at me with no words to say would be a common occurrence.

I walked to the locker room and unlocked Judy's locker like it was any other day. But it wasn't. It was the worst day. A day to face people who knew what I had done. I wasn't ready, but what choice did I have? I suppose ripping a bandage off and getting everything over with felt like the best choice.

Overwhelming emptiness was clutching my throat, trying to choke me. I took a deep breath and chided myself for not handling this better. As her locker opened, my insides froze. Her sweet-smelling fragrance filled my nostrils, nearly knocking my legs from beneath me. I sat on the bench staring into the locker at her belongings: some clothes, perfume, and a few pieces of jewelry. *Why did I decide to do this today? Would they have taken her stuff so quickly?* Another scolding of myself, *Stop it, Donna. You are here, so buck up and do it.* With cold hands, I removed her belongings into a bag and placed the bag in my locker. *There, it is finished. You can do this.*

I dressed in my costume and headed for Pinocchio Village, where we, I mean…I worked. Inhaling deeply to steady my nerves, I got on the elevator up to the kitchen. The elevator door opened, and the five people standing at the stainless-steel prep table directly in front of me, stared in my direction. One person went pale and came to me. She said she had heard that I was killed yesterday. *I wish. Anything would be better than going through this.* In confusion, I looked around, and the others seemed to have the same wrong information from the news.

How peculiar that information that carries such devastating consequences can be so inaccurate. I was hit with sudden recognition of the mysterious incident that happened at the hospital yesterday. When that poor girl was called to identify her sister's body, she saw Judy. I can't imagine the horror of it all. I now understood my mom's strange quiet when speaking with that girl. I suppose Mom assumed that the dead girl was Judy. That information brought a sudden introspection.

Pulling myself back to the present, I let out the breath I had been holding and said, "It was Judy that died." I wondered if they were disappointed. Judy had been hanging out with several of them after work, and I was uncomfortable with their crowd. I knew they all smoked, and I suspected that was not all they did, and I didn't want to be a part of whatever that might mean. Then the questions came. Who was driving, and how did it happen? Hoping for the imaginary hole in the floor to open and swallow me was not reasonable, but…I hoped they would at least be kind, stare, and say nothing like my friends on the road. Through a knot in my throat, nearly crushing my windpipe, I briefly explained and walked away to clock in.

Thankfully, I would only have to work with one coworker, which would be less awkward since I was assigned to Troubadour Tavern, a small restaurant with only snack foods and drinks. It was only staffed by two people this season rather than where I normally worked, Pinocchio Village, which was staffed by fifteen to twenty employees at the front of the restaurant. Focusing on the nameless guests and pushing some trauma from my mind would be easier. I managed about an hour when an employee spotted me across the park and came to "check" on me. The curiosity of people was in no danger of "killing a cat," but it came close to killing me.

With his questions out of the way, I felt hot tears escaping my tired eyes. Leaving the counter for my coworker to manage herself, I escaped to the back to try to pull myself together. I ran into my manager. He was not happy, understandably, and with managerial concerns ruling over compassion, he demanded I pull myself together, saying, "You are the one who decided to come to work today." It was the verbal slap in the face I needed to snap me out of the emotions. I resumed my duties, but I can honestly say I remember no more of that day. I got off work and made it home with no memory of what I did or how I managed to drive twenty-four miles home without a single memory of the drive.

The next few days, I was scheduled to be off, thankfully. The reality was settling in, and I felt so alone. Crying became a part of all my alone time. My dad spoke with the police officer investigating the accident. According to my dad, the police officer said, "All the witnesses confirmed her story, and honestly, I don't think I could have managed the car better than she did." My dad made sure to tell me that a few times. The officer recommended to my dad that I file a suit against the city for not setting up flairs or cones to warn of troubles ahead. The traffic was stopped because there had been a fender bender, and all the emergency personnel were already on the scene. True to every accident you have ever seen, emergency responders cause a plethora of "rubber-neckers," which bottlenoses the traffic. The officer told him to tell me it was a freak accident as if it was supposed to comfort me.

About midday, Mrs. Butler called. Mrs. Peggy Butler, a redheaded middle-aged divorcee with three sons and a heart full of love, had been a high school teacher I connected with in the tenth grade. I spent most mornings in her classroom before school. Often, I would cry and lament about how I could not please my mom, and no matter what I did, it seemed she was always disappointed in me. But not Mrs. Butler. She was different. She was kind and listened without making me feel I was wrong about my feelings. She had deep-set eyes that seemed to see my soul and radiated her love. In school, I was respected by all my teachers, the principal, and about every other adult. But at home, I felt unseen.

Mrs. Butler, however, made me feel heard, seen, and valued. She regularly encouraged me, believing that I was made to be great. She believed I would be a gifted teacher of anything I was passionate about and hoped I would go to college. She said I was wise and a great communicator. Toward the end of high school, she occasionally hugged me if I was a complete wreck about something happening at home. She always had a kind word for me. When I left her classroom, I left knowing I was loved. She was the one person I welcomed a call from.

Her voice was tender as she softly said, "I'm so sorry, Donna." Weeping again, my body convulsed with the torrential flood of emotions. I didn't feel I deserved compassion since it was all my fault, but I desperately wanted it. Her voice felt like a warm embrace filled with love. She had no questions, and she didn't want to hear any details; she just wanted to talk with me about how I was doing. Though I could not speak, she spoke soft loving words. "I'm sorry this is happening, Donna." "Can I pray for you?"

A whispered "Yes," was all I could get out. As she began, I pressed the phone against my face like a lifeline to some unknown strength trying to infuse me with hope. I needed strength to surrender these emotions and keep moving.

She spoke quietly and tenderly as if stroking my hair. My tears, though a steady stream, were less violent. Her words connected with my soul in some strange encounter like a warm bath. I felt comforted, and after a bit, I started to feel…less broken. Maybe I was less hopeless. My crying lessened, and I could hear her. She asked God for "His presence to fill me."

His presence? I didn't understand, but I felt less pain as if a tiny flicker of light slipped into a small crack of my dark soul. My tears slowed, and my breathing returned to a steady pattern.

At Judy's funeral a few days later, I was alone in the crowd. My parents sat to my left in the front row, opposite Judy's family on the other side. Judy's lifeless body stared at me, reminding me of my great loss and greater mistakes. Shame overcame me as trickles of sadness leaked from my eyes. Suddenly, struggling to breathe, I was afraid to lift my face to see everyone in that room who probably hated me passionately. I killed their daughter, sister, and friend.

Finally, it was time to close the casket, and I was relieved, although I was ashamed that I felt that way. I didn't want to look at her anymore as I could not deal with the pain of what I had done. I didn't even want to go to her funeral. Somehow between the pain of her loss and the shame of my involvement, the pain seemed too great. *How could I face everyone grieving and feel responsible for their loss while suffering my own?* It wasn't fair.

The funeral officiant took his place at the front of the small chapel. He delivered his message with words that never landed in my hearing. I felt dead…until one statement stirred me to life. Just eight words of hope. He said, "The most beautiful flower blooms but one season." In some mysterious way, my soul clung to that statement so greatly that I can still hear and feel that statement in my soul more than forty years later. It was a perspective that allowed me to fantasize that someone else had a say in this matter, and it wasn't all about me. It opened me to the possibility that Judy's purpose was fulfilled, and I was not to blame. I hoped his words and these thoughts were true.

I considered asking someone if these ideas were true, but I was afraid. They might think I was trying to justify her death. Maybe I was, but would that be so wrong? I wasn't "chosen" to die yet, so shouldn't I hang on to living? I felt guilty and ashamed that I was ready to believe any lie that would help me breathe deeply again.

If it were even possible, the weeks following the funeral were even harder to muddle through. Fitful sleep would be my lot for many months to come. I woke up many times in hysteria from the constant nightmare plaguing my sleep: Judy was screaming my name, and I watched again as her head lay in my lap and her eyes rolled back into her head. Night after night, I was haunted.

My mom was pulling away from me even more. I wasn't surprised when my dad told me not to mention the accident around her because she couldn't take it. I felt she hated me even though her words said otherwise. I learned that Judy's mom was suing my parents at that time. Hence, my mom's depressed mood and obsession with hiding anything of any value. Looking at all the lives I had ruined…how would I survive? That terrible wreck was attached like a ball and chain to my soul and dragging me down to a dark and desperate place.

Judy's death left a huge hole in my heart that felt like an endless reservoir of pain. Isolation was all-consuming, and I would try anything to fill it. Initially, I became friends with a "bad girl." Denise always seemed happy and the life of the party. I needed energetic and fun people to distract me from my darkness. Besides, she had not been friends with Judy, which was a relief. She never looked at me with looks that made me self-conscious. Though her freedom of self-expression was less than pure and moral, I no longer cared. It wasn't long before I went to bars to drink and dance. I started enjoying a life that numbed my pain.

It was January 1978, and the driving sounds of the disco era were in full swing with the dance beats of the Bee Gees, Donna Summer, Barry Manilow, KC and the Sunshine Band, ABBA, and the like, filling the playlists of the bars. Life was grand…until it wasn't.

One night I was out with Denise, dancing and having a wonderful time with two guys we met at the bar. They were buying us rounds of drinks as we laughed and partied the night away. The next morning, I woke to realize I was in someone's apartment whom I could not remember. I jumped up to look around and found Denise coming out of another bedroom, looking proud of herself. She asked me if I had fun.

I was shaking my head to clear the fog and remember what happened the night before. Blood rushed from my face as realization started to take hold. *How could I? My innocence is gone, and I am to blame.* As if the shame and guilt I felt from the accident weren't enough, I was overcome with torment here in this place. My thoughts condemned me. *How could you? You knew all that drinking was leading to no good. But you didn't stop it. You should be so ashamed of yourself.* I was willfully involved in the drinking, and now the aftermath was my fault again. I grabbed my purse and ran outside without a word to Denise.

Once I was outside, I recognized the apartments and knew I was close to the club. I ran a half mile back to the club where I last saw my car, like a monster was chasing me. The villain inside me was nipping at my soul. *You are a fool.* As I ran, I remembered leaving with some guy. *What was his name? Larry, or Barry, or Gary…What was it? Donna, you idiot.* I was the one that kept doing all these things to myself. My parents would hate me if they knew. They would never speak to me again. When I got home, I told my mom I fell asleep watching a movie with Denise. I felt the shame of a scarlet letter on me when my parents looked at my face. I wondered if they saw it too.

Needing to be away from my parents' constant scrutiny, I moved out six weeks after I turned eighteen. They tried to talk me out of it, but their approach only solidified my determination. Sue, a new fun friend, and I got a town home and began our adult life. It surely came with a financial and moral price, but I knew of nothing else I could do.

After the first month or so and the newness of living on my own was gone, I circled the same dismal thoughts repeatedly like a broken record. My life was a mess, and there seemed no escape. I wanted to go to college, but my father was still not willing to help me go to school. "Dad," I said with a low tone that would not sound argumentative, "my high school teachers think I am perfect for college. I'm a great student." He looked at me, and I knew the answer was final—no more discussion.

What do I do now? The stress was great, and it was eating a hole in me. I was so lost, and I didn't know what to do. I called Mrs. Butler and confessed the mess of my life. She consoled me and told me that one decision doesn't define your life. She prayed for me. But the hole was too big, and I got lost in it.

A few weeks later, I met James. James was a sweet young man that acted as a gentleman by holding doors and pulling chairs out. He was a year behind me in school, but our birthdays were two weeks apart. His kindness warmed my lonely heart, quickly leading to us sleeping together. I felt more alive than I had in a while, but at the same time, my moral conscience was condemning me. My parents' values rebuked me every time I tried to be okay with my decisions. Weeks turned into months, and once again, I found myself calling Mrs. Butler and giving her blow-by-blow of my shameful life. She listened and sometimes got a little preachy, but it was always loving, and I never felt her disappointment in me. It seemed to me it was her tenderness trying to call forth in me better choices. And while she never said I was screwing my life up, I felt it in my heart, and I wanted to earn her approval. So, I started looking for a way to escape my terrible choices.

Mid-June of 1978, I sat in Pizza Hut by the Navy base pondering enlistment. Would that be the escape I needed? I ate my meal silently and stared at the road leading to the base. I had not come to any conclusions when my meal was finished, so I went home. That night I went out with James to see the new movie, Grease. As we waited in line, James asked me to marry him. I never considered love. I just knew marriage is what good girls do. I said yes.

Chapter Four
ACT, DON'T THINK

Spontaneously made choices may result in tough consequences
you are then forced to live with.
—Donna Bess

A week after his proposal, James left for his enlistment in the U.S. Army. We decided to wait a year to marry until his training was completed and a duty station was assigned. However, the war in Afghanistan steered us in a different direction. All military bases were moved to high alert, and even though James was in training, there were rapid changes afoot. One evening, James called to tell me about some changes. If he were married before he got his duty assignment, the spouse would be permitted to be with him. However, if he got the expected assignment overseas before marriage, a new spouse would have to wait until the next assignment, which could take eighteen to twenty-four months.

Because I had moved back into my parents' home and was hating every minute, it seemed obvious we would have to get married by the Justice of the Peace. My parents were not pleased with me either because they were against our marriage. I immediately needed a new residence. The plan moved from getting married in twelve to fourteen months up to tying the knot in four to six months. The exact timing would depend on James' break in training.

One beautiful sunny day, as I was walking in the back lot of Disney on my way to where I was working that day, I was hit with a foreboding thought about getting married so quickly. I knew it was a risk, and I considered calling it off. But right on the heels of that thought was the consideration of the level of embarrassment and potential questions I would face. Besides, I already had a bridal shower and had paid for the plane ticket and hotel for our perfunctory honeymoon; calling off the marriage now seemed like a painful thought. Besides, I didn't know where this initial thought came from, so I brushed it off as cold feet and moved forward as planned.

About six weeks later, I arrived in Moultrie, Georgia, wearing my casual white dress. James greeted me in his dress uniform. He looked so handsome and fit. His face was bronzed from all the time outdoors. His smile went from ear to ear, and the sight of him took my breath away. A short drive to the country courthouse, we got out of the borrowed car James was driving and ascended the steps of the building, arm in arm, into the dank, dusty, old courthouse. Again, that foreboding thought hit. I had cold feet, but I silently chided myself. Smiling, I stepped forward to the judge's chambers, where a very old, tired-looking judge rattled off the memorized vows in about one minute flat. We placed the rings on each other after the vows, a quick peck on the cheek, and the most uneventful, unromantic, understated marriage had been completed. Like a checkmark on a to-do list, we were married. I wanted to cry. I flew home after our weekend trying to be happy, but I cried the whole way home.

James had another break about six weeks later and flew home for Christmas. One morning after getting drunk the night before, he had a seizure. We didn't find out until three months later, but that was the beginning of the end of his military career. But first, he did get stationed in Virginia, and we moved there and set up home as husband and wife for the first time. I hoped being together and away from family, and his drinking buddies in training would be the break we needed in our relationship.

We were young, impetuous, and guided by lust rather than love. The few months proved that lust fades quickly, and I found myself in remorse. Once again, my life felt derailed, sidetracked from how I hoped marriage might have been, and all I could do was to surrender the regretful feelings I had and deal with the reality that was now my life. There were no other choices. I was raised with Judeo-Christian values, and I was unwavering in my belief that marriage is a lifetime commitment with no questions asked.

Sadly, when James had been in the military just a few months, I learned he had become a weekend alcoholic. When he was not working, he had a drink in his hand. I also discovered how much like his father he was. His dad was a lazy, angry alcoholic, who was emotionally abusive to James' mother. These revelations scared me. I wasn't sure I could live as she had. In our home, our plans every weekend were set. James' buddies would come over and "hang" all weekend, drinking, cursing, and drowning in bravado and testosterone.

I was lonelier than ever before, and I became depressed because I had no friends or family nearby. Most of the attention I received was unwelcome attention of a certain inebriated man. He provided an income, and he assumed and often said I should be filled with gratitude. I was empty, and I knew our relationship was meaningless. I wanted desperately to call Mrs. Butler; however, long-distance calls were a luxury we could not afford.

With medical discharge orders in hand, our lives were off to another adventure. Our six-month anniversary was marked with us moving back to our hometown. I was as directionless and disillusioned as I had been since Judy died, but this time I was in a difficult marriage, unemployed, uneducated, with no idea where to start. We moved back in with my parents. Fortunately, we quickly got good jobs with decent incomes compared to most equally unprepared-for-life friends. I was working at an insurance company, and James was working at a gas station and drove the tow truck for extra money. James also quit drinking when we were living at my parents' home, for which I was very grateful.

Weeks after we got our jobs, we moved into our apartment, and sadly, the weekend parties resumed. But this time, I had family and friends in the area, so I didn't feel as trapped. I always had someplace

I could go. Calling Mrs. Butler became more frequent, and on many weekends, I would go to her house and hang out. She was the mother I wished I had. She always had a listening ear, and I loved her deeply.

For our second anniversary, James and I bought a house. It seemed that we could make it after all. James was still drinking away every weekend with his buddies if he was off, but he worked hard during the week. I learned to tolerate it. Don't get me wrong. I reminisced about those foreboding thoughts more than a few times and wondered if there had possibly been a higher power warning me. Perhaps it was Mrs. Butler's God. But what good did this warning do me now? As my dad always said, I made my bed and I had to lie in it.

Routine made life a bit more bearable. Each night when I got off from work, I had time before James got off, so I would stop by my parents' home. They lived three streets from us. They truly loathed James and the life we had. But much to their credit, they held their tongue most of the time. So going there always made me feel like there was a place of stability despite the mess of my life. I needed that dose of consistency! However, one night the visit was different. For an hour or so, all seemed normal, and as my time came to leave, I rose and said, "I'll see you tomorrow."

Then, as if telling me it would rain, Dad made a glib comment that shook my world. He responded, "Well, you never know."

A lump formed in my throat. I asked, "What do you mean I don't know?"

He told me he had been having chest pain all day and he may not be here tomorrow.

Choking the words back, I said, "May not be here tomorrow?" *No, this can't be. Standing in the dining room, he looked like a specimen of a manly man. He is strong, muscular, capable, and will certainly not die soon.*

I looked into his eyes. Though he had commented almost in jest, his face was lined with concern. My dad lived by the Marine Corps motto, "Never let them see you sweat." That expression doesn't mean you are not sweating like a beast; it just means don't worry others or don't show others you are weak. He was not a man given to flippant statements, so I was scared.

Driving the three blocks home, terror seized my brain. Thoughts raced; *What would I do without him? I have nobody who really loves me except him. I wouldn't survive this dismal life if he weren't in it. I can't live if he dies.* With my world spinning, I began to think the most ridiculous thought. *I can't have my father die before I have my first child.* As if driven by some primal maternal urge, I knew I needed to have a baby. What a bizarre thought! Given the shape of my marriage, why would I dare even think such a stupid idea? But what can I say? I went home and told my alcoholic husband I was ready to have a baby. He was elated because he had been asking me to get pregnant since we married. I did not think through how having a baby would fix that issue. Somewhere in my delusional mind, I thought it was necessary. I threw away the birth control.

All the people I knew at work who wanted babies had been trying for months to years, so I expected getting pregnant to take a while. However, four weeks after that life-altering decision, I discovered that baby-making was easy for us. The positive test confirmed we were going to be parents! Both sets of grandparents were ecstatic. I was excited to be a mom. The elation and thought that this was a great decision lasted for about a month.

The anomaly that overtook me then was strange. It was like I was taking inventory of all our life's acceptable and unacceptable activities. Though I rarely drank, alcohol could no longer be tolerated in my home. I'm unsure if it was because I was afraid of the chaos it had already caused in our home or if there was a greater reason. But I wanted it to stop. What was easy for me was not as easy for James. He agreed to not drink at home and to never again come home drunk.

The next item that needed to change was also painful for James. He needed to improve his grammar. I could not imagine my children speaking in a language that earned them the hostility my parents carried for James or the snide comments that people gave James about the fact that he married up. While those things didn't bother me when they were said of him, it would have hurt if they were said of my children. I explained to James my concerns, and surprisingly, he was all for trying to correct his grammar. It turned out he was not a fan of the jokes either even though he always laughed when they were poking fun.

Things were moving along okay until about six months into my pregnancy. The earth shook inside me one night as I lay sleeping peacefully and was rudely awakened to a warm vile liquid touching my elbow. I discovered it was coming from my nearly comatose husband as he vomited in his sleep. The horrific smell of alcohol-induced vomiting was all too familiar, and I knew he had broken his promise to me in the most spectacular way only four months later.

An ire raised in me like a booming thunderous clap as I jabbed my elbow, now wearing his vomit, hard in James' face. Oh, no worries, I didn't break anything, and the red mark disappeared quickly. But it did wake him from his stupor. In his barely awakened slur, he said, "What are you doing?" Can I tell you I saw myself in my own jail and realized how foolish I had been? I wished I had responded differently to that foreboding feeling. I wished I had made many different choices. I recognized my choices had sidetracked my life; surrendering to these choices felt more like a lifetime prison sentence. But here I was—with a life growing in me—all because of an irrational fear that my dad would die. My dad had a case of indigestion that was resolved and only returned randomly.

My instant and insane decision to conceive a child, however, was now alive with promise. A promise of what I was not sure, but I did know one thing. I had to walk this life out, which scared me to death. I knew beyond a shadow of a doubt that there was no way I would raise a child in the home of an alcoholic. The vomit awakened me from my sleep and awakened me to reality. James either will not or cannot change.

I jumped from the bed as fast as a six-month pregnant person can jump from a waterbed. I screamed at the top of my lungs, "Go to the bathroom! Get out of bed and go to the bathroom." Realizing he still did not know why I woke him to such an angry scene in the middle of the night, explosions in my soul had me angrier than I thought was possible! If I had not been raised to control my anger somewhat, I might have taken this time to beat him to a bloody pulp. Again, I screamed, "You had fun last night. You got drunk, and you promised me you would not do that again. But your promises mean nothing. You promise until it isn't convenient, and then you break the promise. Get up and clean up the bed. I am leaving you. I am done with your lies and selfishness. I don't care what you want or what you do anymore. I am done with you, and I'm leaving this sick relationship while I still can."

It was the middle of the night, and I grabbed a small suitcase from the spare bedroom and packed it with fury. *I will be alone now. He has betrayed my trust for the last time.* Tears of regret and hopelessness filled my eyes. *Am I angry at him for never being a person of his word? Am I angry at me because I was so stupid? Or am I angry at my parents for being right when they told me not to marry him?* Trying hard to move, I packed a few things. My head was pounding, my heart was shattering, and I was trapped. I felt like my life was over. I was going to be a single parent, knowing my parents would always be thinking, *I told you so.*

James sat in the bathroom crying, "Don't leave me. I love you." I have to say: it is a most infuriating and pathetic thing to see a drunk person crying and pleading with you. With ice water running through my veins, I quickly grabbed my clothes and toiletries and raced to my car before it hit me. I had no place to go at 2 a.m. I reclined the car seat as much as possible and wept bitter tears until I fell asleep in the front seat. As the sun was coming up, I awoke to the bleak truth. A swollen abdomen and what is supposed to be a joy-filled experience for any couple was anything but that for me. My impulsive emotions had led to this place. *Why did I not think first?*

I looked at my puffy face in the visor mirror and went back inside the house to brush my teeth and apply makeup. When James heard me, he came in, still crying, "I'm so glad you changed your mind."

Through gritted teeth, I spoke in a quiet, broken venomous tone, "I have not changed my mind. I just had no place to go in the middle of the night. But I am going to work in a few minutes, and I will have a plan by the end of the day and will NOT be returning home tonight." I still didn't know the plan, but I resolved to go to my parent's home if needed.

"Give me another chance," he pleaded.

With contempt in my heart, I yelled, "Why? Why would I give you another chance? So, I can prolong my own agony? I will not raise this child in a home with a drunk. I will not put this child in the horror you were raised in. I will take this child and make sure you never see him or her. I love and want this baby, but it is clear you only care about yourself. My dad will make sure that you don't come around." And just like that, his face changed and became ashen as the blood drained. James had just considered the consequence of his drinking for the first time. My dad did not like James' behavior, but he kept silent. If I told him what I had been living with…let's say James had a healthy concern about a potential interaction with my father.

Though my dad was a retired Marine, he maintained his muscular physique partially through owning a construction company. He was respected by everyone who knew him. He would give you the shirt off his back if you needed it, but don't cross him. Please do NOT lie to him. And DO NOT hurt his only daughter. He was not a touchy-feely person, and he kept his emotions close to the breast. However, if you crossed him, you would know it. He was a man of justice. Do not treat others badly or unfairly. James knew that about my father, and suddenly, as if a flash of reality crossed his life, he knew his next words would determine if he ever saw his child.

Right there in our kitchen, he vowed. "I promise you—I will NEVER get drunk again. EVER! You will NEVER have to worry about this happening to you again." As weird as it sounds, I believed he was telling the truth. He was afraid of losing this child in his life. Being a dad was very important to his identity. He kept his word. He never drank more than two beers and would call it quits for the evening. While our life together did not get fixed immediately, there was a more relaxed and joyful existence after that time.

Nine months and one day after that fateful evening when I thought my dad was nearing the end of his life, we welcomed our first child. Mindy was eight pounds, nine ounces, nineteen inches long, and was a healthy, happy joy to me. James was initially a giddy father. However, his exhilaration flamed out quickly, and he rarely spent time off work with us. I knew what James sought was the title of father but not the responsibility.

Chapter Five
SURRENDER

Perfume and incense bring joy to the heart, and the pleasantness of a friend springs from their heartfelt advice.
—Proverbs 27:9 NIV~

Much to my shock, the first year of sweet Mindy's life was a journey into parenthood that I was not ready for. Because I studied early childhood education in college, I was sure I would be an amazing parent. I knew the basic psychology of it, which made me smarter than my parents. What more did I need? Never mind that I only studied those subjects for two semesters; I knew more than my parents did. Neither of them graduated high school, let alone took any college classes.

Imagine my surprise when I wished someone would come to take this child to raise as their own. This tiny dictator demanded my every moment. She cried all the time. Many times, we cried together. Her first birthday felt more like a milestone on the battlefield than celebrating her precious life. I was humbled to discover that I actually knew little about raising a child, and I was failing. I felt like the joke was on me. I had hoped I had what it took to live the parenting life with joy and fulfillment. But I admit, that first year was not looking good.

Providentially, the day after Mindy's first birthday, I ran into an acquaintance from work, and our conversation turned to parenting. Lynette was a kind soft-spoken woman, who spoke with a thick country accent from her upbringing in the mountains of South Carolina. As I discussed my parenting woes, she invited me over the next evening after the kids were in bed. A night out without Mindy sounded like what I needed, so I quickly said yes without checking with James. To my amazement, James was okay with Mindy staying home with him since she would already be in bed.

I was so excited to be going out, even if it was to discuss children. That evening, I sat and listened to Lynette lamenting about her husband, Steve. Lynette had great concerns about Steve's "eternity." I didn't want to interrupt the diatribe of her worries, but I did not know the topic. As I sat and listened, I realized her words could easily be spoken to me. I had no understanding. She presented the gospel, and Steve rejected her invitation to surrender his life to Christ. Trying not to look ignorant of her concerns, I asked questions about his responses. By the end of the conversation, I had one clear thought nagging at me. *If he doesn't accept Jesus, she will not see him in eternity…does it follow…the same can be said of me? Am I going to hell?* To this day, I have no idea why she thought I understood what she spoke about, but at that moment, I was glad when the conversation turned to children, and she stopped being upset.

Driving home, my thoughts turned back to, *Where will I spend eternity?* A distant memory flooded my mind, and I knew what to do for the answers. When I got home, I crept into my room in the dark so I didn't wake James. I stuck my hand into the drawer of the nightstand. *Where is it?* I kept feeling around in the dark for the small three-by-six-inch tract I had received nearly twelve years earlier when I attended a Pioneer Girls summer camp with my cousins in sixth grade. Finally, my fingers recognized the shape. I gently pulled it from its quiet presence in the nightstand and moved to the living room to read it.

I turned on the light and sank into the sofa like I was reading a good book instead of a tiny pamphlet. My curiosity peaked. I wanted to understand what Lynette was saying and why Steve's rejection of this invitation grieved her so. I read the tract from cover to cover. The message was simple:

1. Admit that I am a sinner and I need a Savior.
2. Be willing to turn from my sins and ask God to forgive me.
3. Believe that Jesus Christ died for me on the cross and rose from the grave.
4. Invite Jesus Christ to come in and control my life through the Holy Spirit.

A prayer incorporating those conditions ended with "I want to trust Jesus as my Savior and follow Him as my Lord from this day forward. In Jesus' name, Amen."

I agreed with all those items and prayed the prayer. I didn't feel anything, but I knew I wanted the assurance of not going to hell.

It was a straightforward message; I felt something was happening because I felt hope. I honestly wasn't sure I understood everything, but I wanted to move forward. I was compelled to do the rest of the steps.

1. Go to a local church.
2. Tell someone you know that would be happy for you.
3. Pray daily.
4. Read your Bible daily.
5. Be available to be discipled.

Because I was a self-disciplined person, with only a few hours of sleep since I prayed that prayer, I got up and dressed Mindy and myself in our best "church" clothes and headed off for our first day of church. It is not lost on me that the day I prayed that fateful prayer and went to church was on Valentine's Day, 1982. The day when others celebrate love and give gifts, I was celebrating love and being given the greatest gift of all time.

My first day in church was a bit terrifying. The unknown is frightening, not because I expected anything bad to happen, but because my parents had told me that Christians were hypocrites. Therefore, I was uneasy. I hoped what was stirring inside was genuine, leading me to something good. So, I went, but I wondered: *What was I walking into as I walked through the church doors?* What I read felt real. Attending church was part of following Christ, and I was determined to do just that.

I was greeted by a gentleman who seemed to notice I was like a fish out of water. He was very kind and helped me find the nursery to drop Mindy off. Then he led me to my adult Sunday school class. I moved to the back of the class and took my seat.

Oddly enough, the topic was the differences in salvation experiences. The teacher asked random people to share their experiences. You guessed it, he called on me. I said in a meek voice, "Well, last night, when I got home from a friend's house, I read a tract and prayed the prayer."

A pin could be heard hitting the floor. Several people gasped at the apparent faux pas, and it seemed all the oxygen was momentarily sucked out of the room. The teacher cleared his throat and said, "You just got saved last night?"

I said, "Yes, well, early this morning, actually." Then, after an apology for putting me on the spot, he asked if I would be willing to tell the class how. I was the perfect example of the Sunday school teacher's category of making an unemotional decision for Christ. But, as he said, and as I somehow knew to be true, this decision would be transforming. It felt like it was the best decision I had made in a long while. I didn't need to understand more. This teacher affirmed my decision as he talked about the freedom and the redemption that God's love would bring. I loved the idea of greater freedom even though I didn't yet understand what redemption meant.

After Sunday school, the teacher took me and introduced me to a woman, Norma Grey. She was a tall, older woman with kind eyes. She stood with absolute confidence in who she was. I could feel her energy to care for me with how she laid her hand on my shoulder and said, "It is wonderful to meet you. Let's talk after the service." I took a seat and listened to the sermon to discover more of this new freedom. After the service, I encountered a few girls I went to high school with. One of them was Norma's daughter. While I was talking with those girls from high school, Norma joined us. I could tell they each had a deep love and respect for her as a mothering figure. The easy banter had me immediately pulled in, and I wanted to be a part of this group. Someone in the group handed me the address and time for the group meeting, and I agreed to come. All of their phone numbers were also provided as I handed over my own. It was a good day. I left that very first day with three phone numbers of "church girls" my own age. Feeling some connections already, I was excited to go to the meeting in a couple of days. I sensed that although my life had been sidetracked for so long, I was on the road to goodness. I was starting to understand that my decision to surrender my life to Jesus to take my sins in exchange for His freedom was the answer I needed to fill me with hope and a future.

If you do not have a relationship with Jesus and are curious about what that means, please go to the Appendix near the end of the book and see "A Life-changing Resource" for more information.

Chapter Six
CHANGING DIRECTIONS

May your choices reflect your hopes not your fears.
—Nelson Mandela

Filled to overflowing with hope and joy, I couldn't wait to get home and call Mrs. Butler. I wanted to see her face when I gave her my news that I knew would bring her joy, so I tried to hide the excitement in my voice when I asked if I could come over. Of course, she said yes. When I arrived, she greeted me and Mindy with a smile that always made me feel like I was her favorite person. We took our places on the sofa in her living room, and I said, "I just wanted to tell you I accepted Jesus today."

She was on her feet and kissing me while squealing with delight like a small child getting a great present. She said, "I knew it, I knew it, I just knew you were coming to tell me that." Without taking the time to explain how she knew, she was off the couch embracing me with hugs and a kiss on the forehead. She asked me to tell her every detail that led to my decision and then there were more hugs. Finally settling down, she mentioned that she had some questions she needed to ask.

She was so curious about why I would always call her to tell her every bad thing I did. I would also tell her the good stuff, but she served as my confessional and somehow made me feel I wasn't all bad. I told her that because I could confess my worst evil and she didn't hate me. In fact, she would often say something really positive about my character, like, "You are kind, Donna," or "you are going to do great things with your life, Donna." I felt loved and accepted. She began to see what her love meant to me. With tears of joy and a hug goodbye, I drove home to make one final phone call.

Next, I called Nancy Carter. She was a girl I met who worked at the same place as Lynette. Nancy worked in my department, so I knew her better. I was aware of her church life and her perspective on who goes to Heaven and honestly, I was not very accepting of either of them at the time we worked together. I had previously pretty much shut her out of my life and thoughts. But, nearly eight months after we both quit the company, Nancy invited me and Mindy to her daughter Bethany's one-year birthday party. Bethany was about six months older than Mindy. Needing to connect with mothers my age, I took Mindy to the party. We both had a good time, but there was never any follow up communication or discussion of us getting together again. I was not invested in the relationship, so the lack of connection went unacknowledged. But now, for some reason which was beyond my understanding, I felt I had to call her and tell her my news. Perhaps I felt that way because I knew of no other person that claimed to be a Christian that I could call. I remembered that the tract I read the night before said to tell two people who would be excited. Nancy was so happy. We talked briefly, and then it was time for me to start supper.

I was happy and full. I had more life in me at that moment than I had in all my life. I was hungry for more. I had already arranged with Norma to begin discipleship.

That day, on Valentine's Day 1982, a new path was set. A new life began that offered hope in a place of despair, community instead of isolation, and a place to belong with family. In a single day, I had found a Savior and His true love, a church, new friends, and something to look forward to. Indeed, I was elated.

I availed myself of every opportunity to grow. Mindy and I were inside the church nearly every time the doors were open. Norma Grey, Peggy Butler, and Nancy Carter were constants through every trial and struggle, and there were many. But I learned to walk through them and not get stuck in the mud or to take a sidetrack just to escape. On the day I surrendered to God, He gave me an irreplaceable gift with deepening friendships. I quickly learned the value of these women who wanted my best. They loved me enough to help me not settle for anything less.

Chapter Seven
TRUE COLORS REVEALED

Consider it a sheer gift, friends, when tests and challenges come at you from all sides. You know that under pressure, your faith-life is forced into the open and shows its true colors.
James 1:2–3 MSG

My early Christian life was beautiful and tragic at the same time. On the one hand, I was so excited about learning and growing in God's ways, bringing great joy. On the other, as the only Christian in my and James' families, they consistently challenged and judged me at every turn.

Since early on in our marriage, James tended to go off on abusive verbal tirades, and my new way of life provided increased fodder. He felt I was being "brainwashed by those church people." Because he intended it as an insult, I took it as such. I fought back his insults with a few of my own. I told him I was pursuing righteousness, and he would yell back, "You think you are better than me." I told him I was better than him. He only thought of himself.

As I discussed James' constant complaints and criticism with Mrs. Butler and Norma, I learned some valuable lessons. First, I learned how to agree with him and show him the truth. I looked up scripture to show him why I agreed that I was being brainwashed. The Bible says, "Don't copy the behavior and customs of this world but let God transform you into a new person by changing the way you think. Then you will learn to know God's will for you, which is good, pleasing, and perfect" (Romans 12:2 NLT). Second and perhaps more importantly, I learned that I was being self-righteous—that lesson hurt.

As painful as it was to admit, I truly did think I was better than James. My love for him barely had a flicker of light left in it. Mrs. Butler and Norma taught me many things about how to be a wife. "Wives, in the same way, submit yourselves to your own husbands so that, if any of them do not believe the word, they may be won over without words by the behavior of their wives when they see the purity and reverence of your lives" (1 Peter 3:1–2 NIV). I spent time repenting for pride and asking God to help me love and see James as He does. I admit, loving someone who puts you down is super hard. As I gave my little efforts to God, however, I saw some reward.

I also learned that it was not my job to get people to accept Jesus. My job is to represent Jesus' light and love and let the Holy Spirit do the convicting. That means not responding to their insults with insults of my own. My way of dealing with the hurt had always been to attack back. That tactic is probably not an uncommon one for humankind, but it is not God's way. He says, "If anyone slaps you on the right cheek, turn to them the other cheek also" (Matthew 5:39 NIV).

Regularly, I discussed the messages I heard or the things I read in my Bible with Norma, Mrs. Butler, and Nancy. These ladies represented Jesus well to me. Norma tended to be more direct, and she did not mince words when it came to any correction I needed. Mrs. Butler, having known me for many years by this point, came at discipling me from a different perspective. She wanted to know what I was missing that I was trying to fill with my attitude or actions. For example, she asked me to consider: If I was not feeling loved, was I attacking James out of anger that he did not love me the way I needed? She often tried to point me to the "why" of my actions. Nancy, on the other hand, was my confidant and a great friend. Going through the struggles of life, we became spiritual champions for each other as we grew through our trials, often trying to learn similar lessons. It was wonderful to have the encouragement of these women, and I was blessed to have relationships with these three women in my early development as a Christ follower. As I said, they were my tribe, they became my family, and the ones I could count on.

I was beginning to understand that surrender encompassed more than the first salvation decision I had made. I was learning that the true meaning of surrender was to give up my ways for God's way, and it was an ongoing process. I was slowly becoming more mature, and life at home was getting better. It wasn't great by any means, but at least I wasn't making it worse than it was.

Our new pastor, Pastor Dale, called me into his office two years after I got saved. I was nervous because it felt like being called into the high school principal's office. But what he said was that he wanted me to lead the women's group. I was silently bewildered. *Are you kidding me? Do you know who you are talking to?* My mouth got stuck, which was very uncommon for me. I sat staring at him as if he was speaking German. He clearly didn't know what kind of a person I was or what kind of a wife I was.

He broke the silence by telling me what qualities he saw in me and how those traits would help me become a great leader. I spoke with an incredulous tone, "The group is filled with women who have been walking with God since they were children. They know way more of the Bible than I know. I don't think I can be a better leader than any of those ladies. They have mentored me."

He smiled and said, "Don't let anyone look down on you because you are young, but set an example for the believers in speech, in conduct, in love, in faith, and in purity" (1 Tim 4:12 NIV). He asked, "Can you be an example? Can you do that, Donna? What I see, and Norma agrees, is that you are humble and hungry. That is what it takes to be a good leader. I believe you can do it."

He talked about what the group would look like, how I would go about it, and how he would support me. He said, more than once, that I would be an asset because of my passion. By the end of the conversation, I was ready to think about it seriously. I went home and talked with my tribe. Much to my shock, they each felt it was right for me to take this next step.

I never saw myself the way they did, but I trusted them. I knew they saw the hidden parts of me—warts and all! I spoke with Norma weekly and Mrs. Butler several times a week, and Nancy, nearly every day of the week. If they believed in me, I would take that step of faith and lead the women's group.

To my great surprise, our first meeting was amazing. The ladies that had been mentors were now cheerleaders. They wanted to see me "take my place." Wow! It was such a gift.

Author Bryant McGill said, "Whatever makes you uncomfortable is your biggest opportunity for growth."[1] I have to say that I agree with him.

The growth I experienced so quickly can only be because I continually laid myself before God and said, "I have nothing if you don't do it. Help!" And He did, repeatedly.

Several months into leading this group, my second child was born. Because I was not in church when Mindy was born, I had no women in my life that had babies; no wisdom was shared, and no comfort was provided. But with this child, Christ had come into my life, and I was feeling so blessed. What an endowment of wisdom and generosity I received from all those women. When I brought Jarred home from the hospital, people greeted me and showered me with love, presents, encouragement, and meals. For any issues I had with postpartum and breastfeeding, there were many women with experience to direct me. So, this is what it was like to have a FAMILY. I knew that James had to be taking note of this incredible outpouring of love. We had nothing and nobody like these people in our lives. Despite continuous struggles in our home, my spirit could not be dampened. On Easter Sunday, 1985, I awoke with joy in my heart. After breakfast, I dressed my two children and myself in our Easter coordinated clothes and set off to church. I walked into the sanctuary and found a gorgeous display of flowers on the stage and around the pews. The presentation of color and joyful anticipation of the celebration was a feast for the soul, and it elevated my heart to greater gratitude.

Gleefully, I sat next to another married woman who attended church alone. Before the service started, I asked her how long she had prayed for her husband to receive Christ. Her answer broke my heart and stopped my joy in one fell swoop. For the next hour of the Resurrection celebration, I tried to focus on the words being spoken. But her response played in my mind, *thirty-three years...thirty-three years...thirty-three years*, like a scratch on a vinyl record.

The service ended, and I left to pick up my children from the nursery. As I picked them up, I wanted to weep. Once I was home, I put them down for naps and went to my room. At the foot of my bed, I knelt, broken and sobbing. I was pouring my heart out to Him in prayer, "Lord! I can't breathe. How can I raise these children to love you in an environment that is hostile to you? How can I help them to live a life that pleases You when their father and grandparents will teach them self-interest? Thirty-three years Lord. I have only been praying for three years. I can't make it thirty more. I am miserable. I can't!"

Then I heard God speak to my spirit so loudly that it almost seemed like it might have been an audible voice. With all the tenderness of a Father that held his daughter close, He said, "Donna, who loves those children more? Me or you?"

Of course, the answer was obvious, "You do, Lord!" I whimpered.

He replied, "Then, why worry? I will give you your heart's desire."

I wanted to rejoice, but my overwhelmed emotions wanted to remind Him first, just in case He missed something happening here in my home.

Through a torrent of tears, I lamented, "But Lord, have you seen what I live in? Do you know how hard it is to live here with verbal abuse? James thinks I am being brainwashed and spends nearly every weekend away." I imagine now that God had to be laughing at me because of what happened later that evening.

I rose from my knees and resumed my day with a promise that God was more than able to take care of my children. He would do what He said he would do. I knew I had to trust because I was certain I would have never thought of those words on my own. I had heard His voice.

That moment became a capstone of trust as I raised my children to love God. I now understood that though I thought I was raising them alone, I was never alone. I was beginning to understand the redemptive love of God in a way that brought light and hope where there had been none. The God of the Universe called my children by name before they were formed in my womb. I could not possibly want better things for them than He does. The Bible says: "Before I formed you in the womb I knew you, before you were born I set you apart; I appointed you as a prophet to the nations" (Jeremiah 1:5 NIV). Jeremiah complained to the Lord that he was only a youth and didn't know how to speak. Well, those words fit my bill. I felt like I was in over my head. But, true to His Word, God led Jeremiah to be a great prophet to the nations. That fact encouraged me to believe that God would work in my situation.

A little later that day, my husband came home from who knows where. We had a brief conversation, and then the children woke up from their naps. After an early dinner, I got up to get the children ready for an evening church event, and the most unexpected thing happened. James came into the baby's room while I was dressing Jarred to ask if I would like him to go with me that evening.

Trying to contain my enthusiasm and balance the deep skepticism hidden in me, I said, "Yes," with the tone I would use if he had asked if the sky was blue. *Can this be? Did he really ask me after I spent fifteen minutes weeping today out of hopelessness? Is God answering a desperate plea?* "Of course. I would love that." My insides were buzzing with adrenaline. This man had never stepped foot inside a church before. His family and mine hated the church. His family didn't see Christians as hypocrites as mine did. Instead, the idea that Christians could not think for themselves was what I had heard from James's mouth multiple times in the past three years.

Lost in my thoughts and still busy trying to dress an adorable squirmy six-month-old, James broke the silence and asked me what he should wear. He was color-blind, and if I didn't match his clothes, he would go out in the craziest colored outfits. I told him a pair of jeans and any shirt he would feel comfortable wearing. Several shirts I was praying would not be his choice. Thankfully, as if an answer to my prayer, he emerged in a country-style shirt with pearl snaps, his jeans, and "roach killer" pointed-toe cowboy boots. He was comfortable.

We arrived at church with only a few minutes to spare. I was nervous, excited, terrified, and elated. The service started with a few hymns followed by the pastor's greeting and an announcement that we would watch a short film titled, *A Father, a Son, and a Three-mile Run*. It was an inspiring true story of a father who helps his son train for a three-mile run. Though the son's life had been riddled with setbacks, the process demonstrates the father's great love toward the son and others. In the process, the young man develops the emotional strength to stand in the face of trials.

The pastor followed the brief film with a message about the Father's love and how His love is even greater. Though I was not shocked when I felt prompted by the Holy Spirit to share the gospel with James when we got home, I was terrified. I had gone door to door with a group from church to do exactly that, but they were strangers. In that situation, there was no real threat of either messing it up or feeling rejected.

Wanting to ensure I heard correctly, I put out a fleece. I asked God to provide a tangible sign to prove to me that I had heard Him. I would need the Lord to make it clear if He wanted me to proceed. I said to the Lord quietly as I prayed on the way home, "If it is You, James will not turn the TV on first thing when we get home." Truly, this never happened. He was addicted to that box. I was sure he and my mom shared a "TV gene" that had yet to be discovered.

Fleece in place, we pulled into our drive. I walked through the doorway first with the children and headed to the bedroom to prepare them for bed. To my shock, I heard no television as I was dressing them. A little panic started to rise in me. Another fleece was necessary. "Okay, Lord, if I go into the living room and he is sitting in the orange chair instead of lying on the couch, I will know it is for me to share."

Finishing up the nightly routine, I walked back to the living room, and guess where I found James? You guessed it! He was silently sitting in the orange chair, just waiting for me to come into the room. I knew that I knew; tonight was the night. With a quick prayer, I grabbed a tablet and a pen.

I sat in the black chair and asked him if he enjoyed church tonight. He said, "Yes." I noticed he was chewing his fingernails which he did when he was nervous. I questioned if he understood everything. He nodded, "Yes."

With no words coming from James, I decided to move forward. I asked him if I could share something with him. And again, he nodded his head, "Yes." His quietness was a little unnerving, but I proceeded. I took the pad and pen and drew "The Bridge Illustration" that I learned. James listened intently, still chewing his nails. I moved to explain the bridge between two cliffs, one cliff representing the world and the other is Heaven. The bridge represents Jesus on the cross, with his arms outstretched, connecting both sides. I shared the appropriate scriptures as I explained. When I finished, I looked at him and asked if he would like to pray and ask Jesus into his heart and allow Him to be his Savior and Lord?

He said, YES!!

Tears trickled down my face— in part from relief, but mostly for the joy of knowing my prayers had been heard. James and I could move forward, truly being one. I led him in prayer and then asked him whom he would like to call and tell this good news. He had met two guys from my church playing basketball and called them. They were elated.

And so, it began. We were a couple equally yoked in terms of both being Christ followers. We embarked on a new path forward. Peace filled my soul. My babies had Christ followers as parents. More tears! Hallelujah. I could not have been happier; nothing could steal that from me now. God had rewarded my decision to trust Him. I knew the angels in Heaven were singing.

Chapter Eight
EXPECTATIONS

Unrealistic expectations are the fuel that drives you to bitterness and steals your joy.
—Donna Bess

Do you know that feeling you have when you have longed for something you are convinced will complete your life? Maybe it's a new house, a spouse, a child? I had longed for James to be saved for three long years, and now, I was certain that my life would be complete. I knew having Jesus in our relationship would stop him from being angry. Jesus would make him want to live a life that was pleasing to God. I was excited about this new journey that would surely bless my socks off!

The next morning, I awoke with so much anticipation. We could pray together, read the Bible, and talk about Jesus together. We could go to church every time the doors are open together. It was going be great because I finally had someone in my family that was like me. My home was now a "Christian home." Truly, it was an incredible gift to know that my husband and I would be together for eternity. In my mind I was hearing music and skipping like a child down a beautiful path of enchanted woods. We were finally moving in the same direction. I was blessed.

Much to my chagrin, not everyone who says "YES" to Jesus does it with the same zeal or tenacity as I had done it. About six months after James decided to be a Christ follower, my bubble burst. All my hopes for change were turning to anger and bitterness. I didn't have such expectations before he committed to Christ, but now I had them. *Shouldn't I be able to expect him to change?* I found myself questioning if he even believed.

A few times, I thought it was wisdom to bring up what I thought was right behavior to James. Perhaps he didn't know there is a standard path forward in your Christian life. You read your Bible, pray daily, and discuss what you learn with someone who cares—and that is how you grow in your faith. *Isn't that what that tract told me?* Each attempt at discussing these issues ended with a fight and no forward path. I could not understand why he was transitioning from the ideas of the world to the views of God's Kingdom so slowly. I felt it was so slow that his moving forward seemed almost imperceptible. This realization stole my joy and was taking my hope that we would be a Christian family that would change the world.

Grumbling to my pastor, he responded, "Donna, God is the one who accomplishes the work in others when they give their lives to Him. He doesn't need our help. You need to pray for James."

Oh, brother, I thought. My level of annoyance was great, and I sure didn't want to hear "trust God." I wanted and needed a way to fix the nightmare I was living in.

I continued to leave written out scriptures such as: "Do not love the world or anything in the world. If anyone loves the world, love for the Father is not in them" (1 John 2:15 NIV) around on the kitchen counter, the bathroom counter, and the coffee table in hopes that James would read one and it would impact him.

Reading such scriptures caused a crisis in my soul. James dearly loved the world's way, and still sought prestige, power, and recognition at work. He hardly considered his family or what God had to do with anything. It was as if nothing had changed except James' social life. I wrestled with my thoughts: *How can it be wrong to want change? Am I prideful to want Jesus in my marriage? Am I guilty of judgment because I don't want to settle for anything less? How come I can't just be better at this Christian walk? How come I can't rise above these emotions?*

Between self-reflection, self-criticism, and judgment of James, I felt like I was a mess. I desperately tried to walk in righteousness, yet I thought I was only marginally successful. He proceeded with little change in the first year of his Christian life. He attended church services and even more church activities, but it seemed to me that his motivation was to have a social time with the boys. He had developed friendships with several men who played basketball and softball on the weekends. I thought eventually that some of their godliness would rub off. However, it didn't seem like he had any desire to grow. My resolve was weakening. I was beginning to question the point. Depression was starting to take a deeper hold...again.

I spoke with Norma about James' behavior because I hoped she would get some men to disciple James as I had been discipled. As far as I could determine, that was the thing lacking. James didn't have a "Norma or Mrs. Butler" in his life. However, for one reason or another, the men met for spiritual growth when James was working. He attended randomly, but it seemed like another night of the good ole boys' club. They did have a spiritual discussion and prayer, but James only spoke of the banter and jokes.

Depression had been a constant struggle for me since Judy died. Marriage to James catapulted my depression to new heights, and I often thought about suicide. Not too seriously, but it was a mosquito that swarmed around my head that would occasionally bite. My heart was hurting again, and I was feeling bitten.

I continued to pray for my relationship with James and about his behavior. I longed to feel loved. Determined to move this mountain, I prayed for—or rather begged, preached, and manipulated—every situation. I was doing it all in the name of love, and I would never have understood that I was wrong if someone had said something. Perhaps that is why nobody did say anything. Life was full of trials for me, yet there seemed to be no escape.

As emotional fatigue set in, I felt trapped like the man in an old commercial for Dunkin Donuts. It shows the man going out the door in the early morning, saying in a robotic tone, "Time to make the donuts." He enters back in the door at dark and in the same monotone voice, "I made the donuts." Again, walking in another morning with rain and the same mundane tone, "Time to make the donuts." We see him walking in on another morning when it is snowing, and he says, "I made the donuts." This repeats a few times to make the point the donuts are always fresh, because this man and other employees were always working to make the donuts.

Though I did not use a monotone voice like the man in the commercial had when I spoke with my family, I was stuck in the same kind of routine he was—we both had limited joy. The cares of our home were wearing me out. Financially, I prayed through each week's groceries, trying to feed a family of four with barely enough money to feed one. Bills were late, our marriage was awful, and James was oblivious. His job was to go to work and provide a paycheck. I raised the children, cleaned the house, mowed, and weeded the lawn, took the car to the shop, fixed the plumbing, and homeschooled Mindy. Although I didn't have the power to change any of our circumstances, I just decided to suck it up and keep it moving. Time to bathe the kids. Time to clean the floor. Time to do the laundry. I made the beds; I cleaned the kitchen…Additionally, I was at church two nights and two mornings a week, ministering to others.

I was tired physically, emotionally, and spiritually. I was worn out and feeling ill. Suddenly an alarm went off in my head. I had felt this way before. *No, no, no, no, no, no! It can't be! God, you would never let that be the case. Please, God.* This thought was taking me to my knees. *It can't be true.* Fear swept over me like a flood. Fighting tears, I made it through the rest of the evening with a quick trip to the grocery store before bed.

Nightmares and restlessness stole my sleep as James slept like a baby. I got up, made breakfast, and packed his lunch in the morning. Once he left for work, I went to the bathroom to do the test.

All color drained from my face as the stick turned pink.

Chapter Nine
WHEN ALL HOPE IS LOST

In your righteousness, rescue me and deliver me; turn your ear to me and save me.
Psalm 71:2 NIV

Emerging from the bathroom, I began to wonder. Is it pink because I was two minutes late checking it? But my perfectly regular cycle was off, and that never happened. It had to be correct. I was going to have another child. Although the news was secretly thrilling and equally terrifying, I knew this information would not be well received by James or my parents. My mom, particularly, was critical of my every move.

When James came home, I told him we needed to talk. We went into the bedroom, and I showed him the stick. He looked at me and glazed as if he wasn't sure what he was looking at. I said, "James, I'm pregnant," with a matter-of-fact tone. He asked how this happened. Not that he didn't understand the biology, but our other two children were on purpose, and our birth control had never failed. I understood the question but had no answer. "I don't know," was all I could say.

The next evening, we told my parents. Mom was so angry that "you would allow this to happen." She understood the gravity of another mouth to feed amidst our shaky marriage and poor finances. Still, her anger did nothing to help with the pressure we already felt. We came home with no words. What could be said? It was clear that Mom was not happy. Dad didn't say much. James went to the TV, and I resumed getting the children ready for bed.

For the next few days, barely a word was spoken about the pregnancy, almost as if not talking about it made it less real. It was easier to focus on what was happening before us and not deal with things we couldn't change.

During the next few weeks, we began to accept this new life as a gift. We certainly had no clue how to manage it, but in a rare moment of spiritual reasoning, James reminded me, all children are a gift from God, and this child is no exception. We have enough love to go around.

My doctor finished my exam at my six-week checkup and told me I was not pregnant. At least not six weeks pregnant. I knew immediately that I had made a mistake. When I questioned if the test was correct when I was late checking the result, I should have gotten a second test. But now, I had not been using birth control for four weeks.

My emotions were all over the place. I knew we didn't need another child. But I had adjusted to the idea and was happy about it. I was almost certain James would not want another child if given the choice. Maybe this was the reprieve necessary for Mom to let up on her ugly disposition toward me. Later that evening, when James came home from work, I would have a conversation with him.

In the meantime, I went over all the pros and cons. The only pro was that I wanted another child. The cons list was lengthy. When James came home, I told him about my mental list. As expected, he was not overly upset that I was not pregnant, but he also was not relieved. For that, I was grateful. We discussed that I had not used birth control for the last month and what I should do now. After some time, we decided to let go of this idea of another child and return to using birth control. If God wanted us to have another child, it would have happened in the past four weeks.

Just two weeks later, after another positive pregnancy test and confirmation at the doctor's office, and indeed I was now pregnant. Because of how it happened, my mom was more convinced than ever that I had done it on purpose and withheld her love and support for the duration of the pregnancy and delivery.

I suppose it was her actions that pushed me to the breaking point. Because now, not only did I have an unsupportive husband, but I also had an unsupportive mom. With both her lack of understanding and the raging hormones of pregnancy, depression was taking a deeper hold of me. I hate to admit that she had this kind of power over me, but her disapproval was caustic and burned my soul to the point of causing me to wish I was dead. I thought about killing myself even when I wasn't thinking about it. Driving down the road, a sudden thought would hit me: *Ram that semi, and it can be over,* or *Drive off that embankment, and it will be over.*

I prayed often, but it was as if my words vanished in thin air. Nothing changed. I felt no peace and no presence. I began to wonder if I was even saved. Wishing for death, as I mentioned, was a recurring undercurrent of my life. Most of the time, I could defeat the thought with reasons like, *You can't leave your children; nobody will love them like you,* or *What if you fail at killing yourself and you end up being alive in a vegetative state for the rest of your life?* I knew the last thought was a terrible reason, but unfortunately, it was probably the greater incentive against suicide. I felt someone else could love my children better because I was deeply depressed. But being a vegetable would ruin everyone's life—not just mine.

One terrible afternoon, James had a friend over, and they were lounging in the living room, laughing with a gaiety I had not experienced in many months. Honestly, I resented his ability to push our struggles from his mind. I knew it was only possible because he didn't have to deal with them. Just work, provide a paycheck, and I, the enslaved person, will make it work.

The pressure of mounting bills, limited groceries, and a growing apprehension about how I would manage having a new baby continued to drain me. Making our restricted budget stretch beyond what was reasonable did not bother him in the slightest. James sent me to apply for food stamps, and he stayed with the two children. After all, he was off from his long fifty-hour work week, and he needed to rest. For the previous eight years of my life, anything I did, resulted in his verbal abuse, and now my mom's action added insult to injury. The shame Mom had in her eyes when she looked at me, in addition to her snide remarks when I remotely indicated anything was difficult, seemed to be mounting an attack on my sanity. My escape from my parents' home was a deeper hell than I could have imagined. James saw me as his personal slave. It was infuriating! Rage mixed with complete and utter hopelessness washed over me. Though armed with the Word of God, my fight against negative emotions was failing.

At that moment, I no longer cared about winning that fight. I was ready to succumb to defeat and wave the white flag. Death could have me. I could no longer go on. I needed peace, and suicide was the only way. Thinking through how I could make this happen, it occurred to me the overpass was the key. When I drive off the side, my car will roll over and over until I settle at the bottom. Nobody else would be injured and it can all be over. I grabbed my keys, hugged, and kissed the children goodbye with tears in my eyes, and headed for the door.

Chapter Ten
DRY BONES RATTLING

"For he orders his angels to protect you wherever you go. They will steady you with their hands to keep you from stumbling against the rocks on the trail."
Psalm 91:11–12 TLB

Driving to freedom from the darkness swallowing me, I reassured myself that *the children would be okay. They're young; they will move on. My parents will make sure they are well cared for. I don't need to worry about them. I can't handle this life. James only thinks of himself, and I am drowning.* As I drove, I thought of the freedom just ahead. The overpass was nearing. *I could die without anyone else being hurt. After all, doesn't the Bible say, "To die is gain?" I need some "gain." I am no good at this Christian life thing. I'm on the phone two nights a week, counseling women. God, if they only knew what a mess I am, they would never listen to a word I said. They probably would never speak to me again. I was no more spiritually whole than the closest lost person. It's embarrassing. I am a failure.*

Suddenly nearer to the end, the car radio playing in the background seemed much louder and broke into my ruminations, forcing me to hear the conversation. It was weird because I hadn't even noticed the radio was on even though I had left home almost fifteen minutes earlier. I guess I had been engrossed in my thoughts. However, I then heard the radio host ask, "Did you know there is a study that shows laughter, even if it is fake, can improve your mood?"

Apparently, a study showed that laughter, even fake laughter, can increase endorphins and elevate mood. Laughter from watching funny TV shows has been known to break depression. Pondering what they said and the feeling that God had just stepped into my space in this car with this message, I decided I had nothing to lose and gave fake laughing a try.

After a few moments, the fake laugh turned to real laughter as I considered what an idiot I must look like alone in my car. But I noticed something amazing; I did feel a bit better. Perhaps there is some hope. Maybe I can make it. I felt God heard my desperation, and He would make a way. Somehow, I have to trust that. Deciding to not go through with killing myself today, I drove the rest of the way to the food stamp office, pondering hope.

I arrived at the dismal welfare office, walked through a crowd, put my name on the list, and sat down. Feelings of failure were trying to snuff out my barely flickering hope. I never thought I would be begging for bread. Doesn't the Bible say that His children shall not go begging for bread? Yet here I am. Circumstances again confirm that I am a failure in this Christian life. How do I overcome this feeling?

As if to break into my thoughts, my name was called. The nicest lady asked me to tell her my story and how I came to need food stamps. Quickly, I explained to her that James had lost his job, and, while he does have a job now, we have yet to recover from the time when he didn't have an income. She was incredibly kind, full of joy, and sympathetic to our needs. She looked me in the eyes, and she didn't make me feel like the failure I believed I was. She encouraged me by telling me, "Sometimes things happen that make life difficult, but you will recover. There is always a way; you must have faith." Though her words were few, they were a lifeline. As I thought about her words, "There is always a way; you just have to have faith" something stirred in me. *God, I want to believe there is always a way. Help me believe.*

I left that office with a bit more hope than when I left home that day. I was reminded of the story where Ezekiel prophesied to dry bones, and they came alive (Ezekiel 37:7). I felt that miracle happening in me. I didn't understand how this change was happening, but I knew God had heard my cries and was answering. Because of the kind woman whom I had just met at the food stamp office, we had some help putting food on the table. It wasn't a solution to all of life's woes, but it was a start.

As if the God of the universe said, "I'm not done yet with answering your cries," not long after arriving home, Pastor Dale called. He wanted me to help with something else.

I flippantly said, "If I have one more responsibility, I may blow my brains out." I was not being serious about the "blowing my brains out" part, as I would never consider shooting myself, but he heard my desperation. He heard that I had reached my max capacity. He asked what responsibilities I would like to give up. Without hesitation, I told him, "Everything except the women's group," in a half-kidding and a half-begging tone.

To my surprise, he said with no delay, "Done." No questions. No cajoling.

I hung up the phone in complete disbelief. God had heard me. The loud radio had been talking about breaking out of depression. The food stamp lady had been so kind, and now Pastor Dale removing responsibilities I didn't want. I was sure God was listening, and I knew He was moving on my behalf.

I already felt like I could breathe a little easier, as if the Almighty had breathed life back into me. I could narrow my responsibilities to five-year-old Mindy, my sweet girl struggling with developmental issues affecting our homeschooling; Jarred, our 18-month-old tiny package of dynamite, who raised the roof every chance he got; and the new baby I was carrying.

A few weeks later, there was a conference at church called the "Restoration Conference." It was a conference to introduce us to the power and gifts of the Spirit. Some felt their hearts being broken as they ran for the hills rebuking the teaching as lies. Others felt their hearts being set free and embraced the teaching like water to a dying man. Then there was me.

I was skeptical! I could not decide who I believed. I was taught the gifts of the Spirit were a thing of the past, but after hearing this teaching I wasn't sure. I wrote down all the scriptures they shared and went home and poured over them. I prayed for wisdom and asked God to show me His truth. I asked Him to show me if I had previously believed a lie about the gifts being a thing of the past. I scoured every scripture, including the chapter before and after. I had to understand.

Midway through the conference, Nancy and her husband Gary drove to town to be a part of the conference. She, too, was thrown into the same struggle. We discussed the messages and scriptures and cried out to the Holy Spirit to speak clearly and lead us in His truth.

My heart began to be exposed. I began to see that I had mindlessly followed a teaching that I had no personal understanding of. I never took the time to look it up myself and unfortunately, I had even taught a few new Christians in a small group, the very thing I had been taught. I had such angst about the scripture in James 3:1–2 that says teachers will be judged more strictly. "Oh God," I cried out, "if this is true then I have taught your Word incorrectly." Honestly, I wanted so badly to prove that gifts like tongues, prophecy, miracles, and healing were a thing of the past so I would not be guilty of teaching something wrong.

On the fourth day, the speaker introduced something I believed so easily that it seemed like the Holy Spirit put His stamp on it, and I was stopped short. He discussed principles from a book titled, *The Secret Life of the Unborn Child*. He shared the research presented in the book proving that we are thinking and feeling while in the womb. What happens to a baby in the womb can profoundly shape the people they become. Suddenly, I was filled with the idea that all this "woe is me" emotion I had been living in during my pregnancy was harming the sweet baby in my womb.

Repenting of my self-centered thinking, I asked God to reverse the effects of that junk I had just lived through and protect my baby from any negative consequences. Later that evening, I asked one of the speakers to pray for me and my baby. I renounced all negative words spoken in the presence of this baby and broke off any chains that may have been attached to my baby by my attitude and actions. I knew that I needed to make some serious changes.

The next few weeks following the conference, I spent hours in the Word reading and praying and studying the conference notes. Part of me was still trying to prove these types of spiritual gifts were a thing of the past, but the more I searched the scripture, the more I proved I was wrong. I repented and prayed for those whom I had taught wrongly to receive His truth, just as I had. Nancy and I each came to the same understanding at different times and in different ways. I came to believe that these gifts of the Spirit are for now and until Jesus comes back.

Also, the fact that my words and actions could not only hurt the baby in my womb but damage the children in my home brought an acute awareness. Intentionally and consistently, I prayed for God to change my heart. I worked on changing my speech and attitude. I realized that allowing depressive thoughts was damaging not only me, but those whom I love. I asked the Holy Spirit to prompt me every time I started down the pity party trail and bring correction. When words or thoughts would come to me, true to His nature, I would hear a gentle whisper of the Holy Spirit helping me to change my ways.

Within a month or so after the conference, I did receive a "filling of the Holy Spirit" that was tangible for me. I felt His touch like a kiss as I lay prostrate on the floor. I can't explain the love I felt, but it changed me. One of the greatest changes was my ability to understand Scripture like never before. But another blessing was that never again did I seriously contemplate suicide. Though there have been many hard times and several times when I asked God to take me, I never sought to end my own life after that love encounter with the Living God.

Chapter Eleven
OUT OF THE GRAVE

*Love is not when you see someone's strength and admire them;
Love is when you see their flaws and cherish them anyway.*
—Donna Bess

The first year following that conference brought great changes in James and me, as well as some challenges that were not easy but helpful in the long run. James felt I was expecting too much, that I was too stressed, and lacked contentment. I felt James wasn't hungry for more of God in our lives, and his lack of participation seemed like laziness. There was probably much truth in both of our viewpoints.

The power struggle between two strong-willed people convinced beyond a shadow of a doubt that they were each right is not easy to overcome. Let's say the struggle—which was really about whose desires or viewpoint would win—was real! Eventually, both of us began seeking to walk in wisdom, and each of us was open to learning from the Holy Spirit through training we were receiving at church.

Norma and Mrs. Butler continued to encourage me, challenge me, and help me mature. James and I shared in the trials and triumphs as we hurt and laughed through tough conversations. Okay, I admit, we even continued with some outright screaming matches. In retrospect, we were both living out of our "fleshly" desires to be right. Screaming was a condition of both of our homes growing up, and we accurately reflected that loss of control in our relationship. We began to see that shouting at each other was demeaning and it created a communication style with no winners. And although we wanted to change, it took time. But our commitment was there. We wanted what God had for us, and we were excited to see His plan come to pass.

I still felt I was growing more than James; however, when I admitted to Mrs. Butler how I felt, my conversation with her exposed a few things in my heart. First, I tend to see the finish line and want the result right now. Second, I quickly judge James for not being on the same page as me. To improve these issues, I must be resolute to stop, take a deep breath, and examine who was in control. Was I seeking power, or was I surrendering to God to manage His timing? Neither of those lessons was easy for me, and frankly, I had difficulty not trying to help God get James moving forward more quickly. With great effort, I continually handed James' behavior to the Lord in prayer. God then sent two wonderful people into our lives.

David and Gail Riddle started a drama team at our church, and both James and I joined it. We enjoyed much quality time with Gail and David building sets, studying lines, and hanging out for dinner and games. Eventually, James and David were best friends, and James gleaned much wisdom from David. James' time spent with David challenged him like nobody ever had, and it wasn't long before growth was evident. Their friendship was wonderful for me. I loved having a godly man who could address issues that came up with James and me so that James would receive them. David was a gift from God straight to my heart. He was what I needed during that season of giving James to Jesus.

James' and my relationship flourished with the growth of James' love and devotion to God and therefore to me. I grew to love this man with a depth I had never known. I was grateful to wake next to him each morning and fall asleep beside him each night. We were one flesh with Jesus now. We had grown through the challenges and tough times, and we learned how to lean on the Lord. For example, James was insistent that we cosign a loan for a family member to buy a motorcycle as a cheap form of transportation they needed. I was very against this practice, and so I read James this scripture: "Don't agree to guarantee another person's debt or put-up security for someone else. If you can't pay it, even your bed will be snatched from under you." (Proverbs 22:26–27 NIV). I told him we surely could not afford to pay that debt, and he told me there was no way we would be stuck with it. Not dissuaded by my reasoning, James insisted we move forward. Seeking to honor him as my husband, I agreed to cosigning for the loan.

The person for whom we cosigned, lost his job and because he had no income, he stopped paying the insurance. Suddenly, the vehicle was stolen, and guess who had to pay for the loan? If you guessed us, you are correct. It was a valuable lesson for me to be quiet and not say "I told you so." It was so hard! But instead, I said, "Don't worry, we will get through this—God will make a way." The next week at church, James shared with other men how he had learned to trust his wife's wisdom moving forward. He had made a mistake, and he told them I was gracious about it. These types of lessons moved us into a wonderful and supportive relationship. We became leaders in the small groups, and we ministered well together.

Our family was blossoming with goodness, and we laughed much more as a family. We enjoyed our now twenty-month-old, four-year-old, and seven-year-old children. There were many family fun nights following dinner at the table instead of in front of the television. Despite the many hard times we were still going through, life was wonderful because we did it together.

As our tenth anniversary approached, James and I decided to do a wedding as a vow renewal. Our budget was tight, but we pulled together a wedding with bridesmaids, flower children (our two girls), a ring bearer (our son), and groomsmen in about three weeks. I made all the bridesmaid dresses, and I found bargains for the kids' clothes. Our church pastor, Pastor Dale, was our wedding officiant.

We had such a special day of celebration. Standing arm in arm with my dad, he walked me down the aisle—something that had not happened since we had gone to a justice of the peace when we first got married. My tears wanted to give way to the overwhelming gratitude; I could not shake the thought that less than two years before, I had lost all hope and believed there was no point in living. I was standing here in a white princess dress, ready to recommit my life to God together with my husband, whom I loved deeply. The blessings of the Lord were chasing after us and we were basking in His love that had not only redeemed our lives, but also renewed our love for one another. God had made a roadway in our wilderness and this moment was holy.

Mom was sitting in the front row trying to corral Jenna, who would not keep her place as a flower girl. I knew my mom had been angry that her only daughter had not had a wedding, which certainly had not made up for that loss, but I hoped she would feel the emotion of this day and rejoice with us.

The music started, and my dad led me forward. I know it is unbelievable that after we had been married for ten years, I felt the excitement of a new bride. We had fought through the trenches. I was now beside myself with joy because of the wonderful gift I was receiving as I re-married my best friend. James was my best friend! I need to say that again…JAMES WAS MY BEST FRIEND!! Just two years before, I had been ready to give up everything. Wow, God is so good. I felt such gratitude that God rescued me from the pit of hopelessness. I could only imagine if I had killed myself and missed out on this redemption.

What a special day it was. Friends and family gathered around us at the reception, telling great stories, pronouncing blessings over us, and sharing a potluck prepared by all those who came to love and share in our lives. They prayed for continued blessings and growth. It was special to have all my favorite people witness this beautiful occasion including Mrs. Butler, Norma, Mom, Dad, and Nancy. What a pronouncement of the faithfulness of our loving God.

Despite all of life's complications, we had joy—a different emotion from being happy. It was an inner knowing that everything would be okay. I learned that while I did not know what tomorrow holds, I could be confident in the One who holds tomorrow. I don't have to understand how life works. I know I must believe in the One, who causes "everything to work together for the good of those who love God and are called according to his purpose" (Romans 8:28 NLT).

Our family had a deep inner peace. When the five of us were home, we still had the normal struggles of the day-to-day. Children still fought one another. They still had times of arguing with their parents, and James and I still had occasional conflicts. Life did not look much different overall, but in some ways, it felt like a completely different world. James and I had become partners. We discussed what we saw God doing in our personal lives and the lives of our precious children. I was no longer raising our family alone. I had a teammate to go through life beside me. God had done great work, and we were bathing in the light of it.

As a family, we were at church so often that our children had sleeping bags and lunch boxes to carry with them. We worked tirelessly on every project. I now had resumed ministry over a few women's groups and leading ministry teams. Occasionally I even went on ministry trips to minister in other churches. Our lives had become about "impacting the Kingdom." That is until...

Seeker Sam and Seeker Sally came to live in our church.

Chapter Twelve
CHURCH CONTAGION

See to it that no one takes you captive by philosophy and empty deceit, according to human tradition, according to the elemental spirits of the world, and not according to Christ.
—Colossians 2:8 ESV

Although the changes at home were amazing, and I was super excited to see how God was moving, I was apprehensive about the way things were going at our church. I loved the leadership, and I wanted so badly to believe in the new path that the leadership was embracing. A few people I spoke to told me I needed to trust the leaders to hear from God.

The doctrine taking over our church came from Willow Creek Church. They called it Seeker Harry and Mary; we renamed it "Seeker Sam and Seeker Sally," but the intent is the same. The idea was to remove everything that could make an unbeliever uncomfortable, get a coffee bar, brighter lights, better sound, and sell this thing. Don't talk about the blood of Jesus, water down all worship and remove any Christian lingo.

Doing some soul searching, I had questions for the Lord. *Why do I find trusting them in this new direction impossible? Do I not trust You to speak through them? Is that what You call me to…blind faith in man to follow You, and I don't question? Does that imply that I don't hear from You or that I need to keep silent and just pray for leadership? I disagree! I can't see a precedent for this new direction anywhere in Your Word. I realize every decision in our life is not spelled out in scripture. They say it is to help the unchurched people come to you, Jesus. But…is it You they are seeking? It doesn't sound wrong to want to get unchurched people in the door. So why am I struggling? But the spirit of this feels so bad to me. Am I wrong?*

Although I can't say it is a contradiction to God's ways, are demographic surveys and market analysis really necessary? If you want to know about the people in your community, why don't you go out and meet them instead of always staying tucked away from the people you serve? Another thought occurred to me. *Am I offended?* When I found out they wanted to target people that were professional families, it told me they didn't want me. I am lower class and uneducated. *It isn't enough that we are faithful servants in the church?* I thought of the following verse: "My brothers, show no partiality as you hold the faith in our Lord Jesus Christ, the Lord of glory." (James 2:1 ESV).

God, this struggle has me in knots. I know those with education tend to seek others of likeness, but where does that leave those not in that class? Should socioeconomic class play a part in building a church? Would it not be prudent to have those of all categories? Please, lead me. James does not have any issues trusting the locomotive to change. But then, why would he? He plays ball with half of the leadership men, his buddies. Truly, I am not opposed to looking for ways to grow a church, but remove all references to the blood of Jesus, the gruesomeness of His sacrifice, like the scripture "by His stripes I am healed," or any word or phrase that could make the unchurched person uncomfortable? I don't understand. How can you take communion? How can you have Resurrection services? How can you be saved, healed, or free? Aren't these critical points? Are we trying to reach the lost without talking about the gospel?

Because I didn't feel I had any answers, I took some of these questions to the pastor and the leaders. They were not receptive to my questions. They just insisted it was the path that "The Lord" was leading, and I needed to accept that.

Potentially walking away from church is so hard. These people were family, who also happened to be leaders of my church. They inferred that I had no idea what I was talking about. It hurt, and I didn't feel heard, and although the pastor did not directly say the following words, it seemed suggested that I needed to get in line or get out. Surely, your family would not treat you this way. My entire Christian life had been in this church. I had been ministering in and outside this church as part of a team for several years. My husband and two of my children were saved in this church. *How was I supposed to reconcile these feelings or convictions with the idea that my leaders didn't want to discuss them?*

I felt Norma was drinking the Kool-Aid and thought I was the crazy one for not seeing it was delicious. Therefore, I took much of my questioning and lamenting to Mrs. Butler. Although she had no answers, she encouraged me in my pursuit to follow God. She prayed with me and for me. She believed in me, and she thought that I heard God clearly. She believed He would show me the way. She never defended the path they were taking, but neither did she criticize it. She continually pointed me to Jesus. I will always appreciate her wisdom.

I mentioned my concerns about this new direction in my small group, hoping others could enlighten me. It seemed some thought it was good to change things up. You know, don't get trapped in the same ole same ole…Some saw the benefit of getting unchurched people's butts in the seat. Some had no comment, and others essentially said, "It is what it is," or "Let's get back to the subject at hand."

In frustration, since James could not agree or validate me in any way, I chose to stay home from church. I felt I could not be a part of what was happening. James accepted that, but he said he and the children were going to continue to attend. I agreed, but it felt awful to be home while my husband took the children to church. I didn't like this feeling, and I prayed that God would do something to get us back into agreement.

A month went by, and Norma came to see me. She wanted to know why I stopped coming to church. I explained my dilemma, and surprisingly, she said, I understand what you are saying. I can't say that I feel the way you think, but if you can't attend this church, find a church you can attend. Just go to church. That was freeing, but I was unwilling to participate in church again without my husband. Since James was still committed to staying at that church, I stayed home and watched church on TV.

Another month passed, and my dear friend and drama team leader, Gail, asked me to come back for one night to do a celebration in honor of Pastor Dale for his seven years of service to the church body. It would be a night of skits and would be fun. Besides, she needed me. Initially, I said no, but she presented it as a "last hurrah," as the drama team will end after that night's festivities.

It turned out that several in the church were feeling the way I was, and one of the associate pastors, Pastor Jason, was leaving the church to start a different church. Gail and her husband, David, were among those leaving. I agreed to come to the event. After all, I wanted to honor Pastor Dale.

Pastor Dale was filled with charisma and very passionate about God. He always taught me to question what was said and to listen to the Holy Spirit. He encouraged and stretched my faith and helped me develop in serving and helping others. I wanted to bless him for all the teaching and training he had poured into me. And, as I had learned that Pastor Jason was leaving to start another church, James and I would most certainly follow as Pastor Jason was one of James' closest friends. Blessing Pastor Dale beforehand felt like the right thing to do.

Walking into the sanctuary turned theater, the room was filled with round tables with eight chairs each. Along the wall were rectangular tables lined up the length of the wall and decorated for this celebration to receive the desserts many had agreed to bring. Happy music was playing to set the tone, and I took my place at the door to collect tickets and hand a program to our guests as they came in the door. The excitement was palpable.

Joy filled the room as cast members moved about the area making finishing touches. The hours devoted to making this night magical were all worth it. We worked tirelessly to memorize lines, rehearse, create smooth and seamless transitions between skits, and build sets.

It was a big evening and an excellent way to end my time at this church. It would make such a wonderful memory.

The doors opened, and I stood ready to greet the guests and give directions for the evening. I was greeting each guest as if they had entered a posh theater with my vain attempt at an uptown British accent. It sounded much more gutter rat cockney, but it was good for a laugh as people moved to their seats, already primed to enjoy the evening. Pastor Dale came through the door; I greeted him with a smile and the same shtick explaining the plans for the evening. Unmoved by my joy, he said, "At the night's end, I need to speak with you." Admittedly, this was a cause for concern. But I had hoped he wanted to discuss why I had fallen off the planet. I hoped he wanted to see how I was doing. I hoped!

The evening was amazing, and the cast knew we were blessed to have been a part of something that was a gift. The crowd was alive with joy and laughter, and many times, enjoyment was heightened with belly laughs and tears, forcing the cast member to hold their line so it could be heard over the cacophonous joy.

As the evening was winding down, it was time to start "tear down" and prepare for the cast party. The party after the show had always been the most enjoyable part as we would sit around laughing about mistakes, recounting great covers, as well as our forgotten and stolen lines. We were a family that fully supported one another, and I knew I would miss this. But I knew it was time to go.

In the back, removing items from the green room to the drama room across the hall, Pastor Dale, and an elder, Rod, were walking down the hall. It was dark except for the light escaping from the green and drama rooms.

I smiled and chirped, "It was a great night, wasn't it?"

They smiled, "Yes."

I responded, "Have a good night. Hey, do you still need to speak with me?" He said yes, and he directed me into a dark empty classroom next to the drama room across the hall. He and Rod walked in, and we stood just inside the door with only the faint light from the hall bleeding in.

It felt weird and awkward to be standing in the dark room like a clandestine meeting. But Pastor Dale did not mince words. He said, "You have been spreading a bad report. You must pack all your stuff, leave this building tonight, and never return." Those words shattered my soul as I stood stunned. My spiritual father believed in me and had walked with me to see me grow. This man was the one who officiated our wedding vow renewal, and I had trusted him. I had no breath. My mind and mouth were frozen as the two men turned and left without another word. I stood very still for a few more moments, trying to process what had happened.

Suddenly, squatting to the fetal position, a wail from my soul gushed forth from the depths. I had no words. Just a death rattle that came forth from the deepest recesses of my being. I could not move. After a few minutes, James came in. He came looking for me as the cast party was starting. The wailing sound carried down the dark hall led him straight to me.

Grabbing me in a tight embrace as if he could somehow pull me from the pain, he tried to coax an explanation from me. "Tell me what is wrong." I stood in his embrace for a couple of minutes as the shock waves wrecked my body, allowing his comfort to bring a semblance of composure.

When I could speak, I told him about the quick, harsh declaration that forever changed my life. Equally horrified, he knew I was in no shape for the cast party, he took me to the car. He went inside to tell the team leaders, Gail and David, that we would not be there for the cast party.

Sitting in the car locked in a gut-wrenching wail, the back doors to the church opened, and James, David, and Gail emerged. They stooped at my feet, still connected to the pavement outside my car door and prayed until I could calm myself again. Gail spoke first, "James told us what they said to you; What else happened?"

"Nothing," I said. "I came out of the green room, and Pastor Dale was walking with Elder Rod. I asked Pastor Dale if he still wanted to speak with me, and he led me into the room next to the drama room. He didn't turn on any lights, we just stood in the dark room with the door open for light. Pastor Dale said one quick demand and then turned to leave. I briefly said, 'It isn't true,' when he cut me off and said, 'Uh-huh,' with a tone that told me to say nothing else, and he turned and walked out of the room with Rod on his heels."

Both Gail and David prayed though I don't recall any of the words in their prayers. They hugged me and James, and I drove home. I don't remember what happened the rest of the evening either, except for the ridiculous amount of crying and a loss so great I could not find words. Pastor Dale, my mentor and friend, had contempt for me and I had no idea why. I was broken. Thankfully, because we expected it to be late, our children were already staying with my mom and dad.

Incredulous as it might sound, we received a phone call from the church the next morning. James took the call, and they asked James to mow the church lawn. He explained that we had been kicked out. That person responded, "No, Donna is not welcome, but you are." The hurt intensified when James told me that and burst forth in a fresh new wave. He held me tight and let me weep for the umpteenth time. I could tell he was seething with anger at their callous attitude, but he said nothing. He just tried to console me.

Negative thoughts and healing scripture competed for space in my brain. As I was telling myself, *I will be okay because God is bigger than this nightmare,* the tormentor was yelling in my ear, "You won't make it; you're not a strong enough Christian, you should have spent more time in the Word, and then you would be ready for this test, but it's too late. You should have kept your mouth shut."

Again, as the tears welled up from deep in my soul, Mrs. Butler was the voice of reason. "What do you think God is doing, Donna?" For several days, I vacillated between healthy, godly thoughts of God's greatness and condemning destructive thoughts seeking to suck the life from my soul. I cried out to my Father, my Redeemer. *Help me see. Help me know if I am in error.* Reading scripture seemed a fruitless ritual until one morning when my eyes beheld this verse...

> Brothers and sisters, think of what you were when you were called. Not many of you were wise by human standards; not many were influential; not many were of noble birth. But God chose the foolish things of the world to shame the wise; God chose the weak things of the world to shame the strong. God chose the lowly things of this world and the despised things—and the things that are not—to nullify the things that are (1 Corinthians 1:26–28 NIV).

Fresh as the morning air, I felt hope breathe upon my soul. I could see myself in this verse. Certainly, I am not wise by human standards; I am not influential, and I am not of noble birth, BUT GOD. God chose me. He doesn't see "worthless"; he sees priceless. He doesn't see "not enough"; he sees more than enough because of His Blood. I am an OVERCOMER! I would overcome these trials. I just need to stay focused on Him, and I will make it through. I am His daughter.

Besides, Dale is just a man. My family is made up of many people. Half the church has been in my home for a meal or a shared experience. I am not alone. I will be okay.

That was until....

I got a phone call from a friend when the Wednesday evening service finished. Pastor Dale told the church that I was unrepentant and that they had to break fellowship with me. They were being asked not to have a relationship with me. Just like that, in a few short days I went from being loved to cut off like some horrific virulent virus that is so contagious the very thought of getting near me would send fear to an unfortunate soul. This information cut through me like a knife. I asked what I was unrepentant about, and he said, "Spreading bad reports."

Nobody had ever confronted me about anything I had done or said. Yet, they skipped all the steps laid out in scripture and treated me as a pagan. While this scripture didn't take away the hurt, it did help me see that I did not deserve this dreadful action. Perhaps I should not have spoken with my care group about my concerns. But even with that, nobody ever said a word to me in the form of correction. But it seemed clear I could not carry this burden and get healed. Very slowly, I started praying for forgiveness. "Lord, I am choosing to forgive; help me walk in the freedom of forgiveness." I won't lie; I struggled to forgive as the loneliness with most of my relationships stripped from me was heavy in my heart.

Mrs. Butler, accustomed to my emotional lament, listened and prayed for me. God bless this woman who stood beside me, no matter what. She was always my champion and quick to encourage me about what God was doing in me. She breathed life into me in some of the darkest places.

But during this dreadful time, Mrs. Butler learned her breast cancer was back, and her prognosis was less than favorable. Suddenly, my issues seemed small, and I didn't want to burden her. Do you know what she told me? It breaks me now, even as I type. "Donna, I am privileged to be a part of your life. Don't hide your pain to protect me. I am fortunate that you trust me to be open and honest as you work through these trials. You teach me more than I give to you." *Lord, Could I just be like her?* I prayed for her to be healed. I prayed against the doctor's curses and believed she would be healed as before.

About one month after being kicked to the curb, Pastor Jason started his church. The initial meeting had about thirty to forty people, most of whom came from Pastor Dale's church. As one might expect, there were conversations about what drove each person to leave. I remained silent, not wishing to comment but, more importantly, not wanting to hear their comments on my plight. Besides, it wasn't as if the details were not already known. It turned out I was the talk of the town. Despite my silence and desire to stay hidden, someone piped in with his perspective of what happened to me and why. He concluded that I was the scapegoat to control the narrative about why people left.

Wanting to reject that person's conjecture, I hoped Pastor Dale would not inflict such harm on me for his ego; however, I could not shake the fact that this idea of him using me a scapegoat made more sense than him believing the lies that he spoke to me. I had been incredibly faithful to serve every time and everywhere I was asked for seven years. This idea that was planted made moving past the great distrust of church leaders so difficult.

But amidst this great tragedy, there was a greater joy being unearthed. James saw me ravaged in pain, and he was compelled to cover me. He began to take on his role as my protector, and he wouldn't allow anyone to talk about me in his presence. He believed in, honored, loved, and saw the gifts within me. He became a champion in my corner when I was breathless from the sucker punch to the gut.

Our marriage, which was undoubtedly good by this time, became more joyful and profound. I had to lean into James because I felt so emotionally debilitated. God blessed him with the ability to see me beyond what I currently believed about myself. He wanted me to succeed in the callings of God on my life, and he was determined to help me get there.

The first six months after being kicked out of my old church were very tough. When I was in the grocery store, "friends" would turn their backs on me…It hurt so badly. The fact that I lived in the same neighborhood as many from that church kept the pain alive and active. I spent much time praying and lamenting with the Psalms. Honestly, I knew I could not relate to the trauma of King David, but my emotions were accurately reflected in his words at the time, particularly by two verses in Psalm 64. "They sharpen their tongues like swords and aim cruel words like deadly arrows…But God will shoot them with his arrows; they will suddenly be struck down" (Psalm 64:3, 7 NIV). The fury I felt at the injustice happening to me was beyond words. Suffice it to say, I was not doing well with the isolation. I was struggling with depression.

Quite honestly, I did not want to go to church ever again. It was so painful. Church was a reminder of all that I lost. But I knew I needed it. So, I went to church every week because I hoped it would help me get through this dark tunnel. I saw church as a dose of medicine. It was a nasty dose in my mouth, but I believed it worked for my good. Those who knew my story were kind, and they would occasionally pray for me.

One person was most memorable. Gail's husband, David, became an elder at this new church. His tender heart touched me as he would speak ever so gently about believing that God has something more significant for me. He asked me to pray for someone once, and my face showed hesitance. He looked confidently at me with his big blue believing eyes, and I moved forward and dared to be used again. His confidence in the Lord using me is when I realized that ministering to others may be the only step forward to get me out of the dark place that had been consuming my soul.

NEW PERSPECTIVE

One thing that breathed a little life into my heart even though it was tough was helping Mrs. Butler. The chemotherapy was rough on her! She was in bed on chemo day and the day after every week. Then a slow ascend to feeling better just in time to start chemo again. I hung out with her as often as I could. Watching her suffer was one of the worse things I had ever seen. Talk about getting a perspective on the challenges in life. One beautiful day, she invited me to shop with her. She was ministering on a retreat with her church and wanted to buy some new clothes. She had lost so much weight that her clothes no longer fit well.

I learned so much about grace by being in her presence. She was so gracious and kind even when she felt like hell, to put it bluntly. She did not complain. Instead, she built up everyone around her. She was an absolute picture of God's beauty, and the last year and a half of living single and struggling to care for herself in complete weakness was a tragically beautiful God encounter.

On December 30, Mrs. Butler succumbed to cancer. Nineteen years had elapsed since the first day I walked in and sat in her classroom. How quickly she grew into the confidant that would end up being used to love me back to life in the darkness I had known. The woman that had mothered me more than any other was gone. Her fingerprints are forever on my soul, and her mere remembrance brings tears of gratitude for every moment I got to share life with her. She was and is an oasis in my life. Oh Father, help me be that for others! She poured out a love that genuinely was unconditional and without judgment, filled with hope and encouragement—a true love that only the blood of Jesus can bring.

I was also filled with tremendous gratitude that my marriage was healthy, and this significant loss did not leave a great void that shook my faith. It is a true testament to the faithfulness of God, who went before me and sent a woman to lead me into a place of peace so I could stop running enough to be caught by Him.

Seeing her suffering allowed me to put some distance between myself and my own grief, which now seemed so trivial compared to this incredible grace she demonstrated under extreme anguish. I also learned about her hurts from a couple of close relationships in her final days, which she never allowed to sidetrack her from what God had called her to. She had learned to walk like the daughter of the King. I long for that to be true of me for the rest of my life.

I focused on walking in forgiveness. T.D. Jakes says, "I think the first step is understanding that forgiveness does not exonerate the perpetrator. Forgiveness liberates the victim. It's a gift you give yourself"[2] Every time I felt a pang of anger or hurt rise up in my soul, I asked the Father to cover the hurt with His love for me so I could forgive and love those who hurt me.

Over time and with purposeful and deliberate steps, I healed. I became functional, and I began walking in joy. I remember the first time I saw one of those "old friends," and I did not feel the same burn. I had released them from the responsibility, and now I felt a little sorry for them. Almost one year later, I was moving on, but they were still stuck with the idea that they had to avoid me.

One time I saw a husband and wife on the aisle in the grocery store. I walked up the opposite aisle so they would not see me coming. As I rounded the corner, I pretended to see them for the first time. With great joy, I said, "Hey, you guys. So good to see you." There was a flash of, *What do we do now?* on their faces. But the husband responded first, and the ice was broken. We talked briefly, but it felt like a miracle.

During the next year, I received apologies from several friends who knew they had hurt me. Only one said more than, "I am sorry."

My neighbor, Jules, said something like, "I am so sorry I hurt you. When we had the meeting, I felt trapped and so weak. We decided because we were weak and not because we believed what was said."

I had already forgiven Jules. However, the release she received as she apologized to me was for herself. I forgave everyone involved by name, whether they asked or not. I let go. I knew it was the only way to heal. For me, the release of unforgiveness came gradually, but eventually, it happened. I was now beginning to get stable footing and growing more and more comfortable with my life, my family, and my relationships.

Only seven months after Mrs. Butler moved her residence to Heaven, I was hit with another catastrophic though insightful crisis. I would witness suffering up close and personal pain again. My dad was diagnosed with esophageal cancer, which the doctors believed was related to Agent Orange that he was exposed to in the Vietnam War. Because the Vietcong could hide so well in their thick, dense forest, the U.S. Military sprayed the forest with Agent Orange to kill the trees. Unfortunately, this led to a cacophony of disease for both U.S. servicemen and non-combatant Vietnamese. This dreadful news hit our family hard as my dad always seemed a picture of health. We had even joked that he would live forever.

My dad showed me a different picture of suffering. Unlike Mrs. Butler, who had a beautiful relationship with the Living God, my dad did not know Jesus. I tried to talk with him several times, and he just said he was glad I had people to watch out for me. Though he was suffering, he didn't discuss it, show it, or even acknowledge it except for an occasional grimace. He did not miss work unless it was for a doctor's appointment. This is probably too much information, but it is indeed the most incredible testament to my dad's tenacity to "never surrender." The chemotherapy he was taking caused diarrhea, and he would take empty milk cartons to work. If he happened to be on top of a building, and not have time to climb down and get to the porta-potty, he would use the milk carton.

Christmas Day, Dad was looking grey and emaciated. He hardly ate a bite, and the pain was etched on his face. Again, he did not complain. By evening he was asking to go to the hospital, which should have been my first clue, since he wouldn't ask for help. Driving to the hospital down a bumpy road under construction, I hurt internally for him with each bump. My dad never came home from the hospital. He died two weeks later.

This seemingly tragic story, however, was more glorious than words express. My cousin, a nurse in the same hospital, came down on her lunch hour to speak with my dad. She asked, "Uncle Don, if you died today, do you know if you would be going to Heaven?"

As I stood holding my breath and praying the most desperate prayer, he said, "No."

She followed, "Would you like that assurance?"

He responded, "Yes." She shared the gospel with the sweetness of her Father calling out to him from Heaven. My dad said he wanted to know that love. She prayed with him, and we rejoiced. My dad received Jesus as Savior and Lord the day before he passed. My pastor had the opportunity to pray with him as well. Glory be to my most excellent Father. My dad and Mrs. Butler are waiting for me when it is my turn to move my residency to Heaven.

Chapter Thirteen
TRUSTING

For I know the plans I have for you declares the Lord,
plans to prosper you and not to harm you,
plans to give you hope and a future.
Jeremiah 29:11 NIV

Just about two years after I started attending our new church, a prophet named Kent came to serve there. Because his looks and mannerisms were so much like Pastor Dale, who rejected me, I found myself constantly hiding. Clearly, these actions were not those of the healed person I believed myself to be. This hiding was difficult since I was a staff member, and he was ministering to various people in the church office where I also spent much of my time.

I only spoke to him when I was spoken to, and I tried to stay busy and keep away from him. On his second to the last day, he asked me if he could meet with James and me. What could I say? I didn't want to, but clearly, I had an issue that I could not deny. I called my husband and asked what he thought, and he was all in. Ugh.

The next day was our time to enter the quaint little counseling room. As we sat, I held tight to James' hand, feeling that he would somehow steady my world. I couldn't say what was wrong with me, but I knew something was amiss. Pastor Kent seemed kind, and everyone who had come in and spent time with him left feeling blessed by him. They shared testimonies of his accuracy and the compassion he ministered out of. Why did that not bring me comfort? I suppose the obvious answer is that my trust factor was damaged, making me feel vulnerable.

The first couple of minutes was him telling me he was aware of some of the things that had happened to cause the church to split. *Church Split? Is that what it was being called? Okay, whatever they call it, he knew about it.* He talked about all the people that had been hurt, and he wanted to help. So, after a few minutes of that, he began to pray.

I can't say I was moved. I wanted to be kind, but I felt angry that he could lump me with the others who left because they were unhappy. Lord. That was certainly not the case with my exit experience. Just as I was writing him off, he moved closer and knelt before me. With tears in his eyes, he repented (in proxy for Pastor Dale) for saying a few things to me that he could not know from someone else since I never told anyone, including James. I was paying attention now because I never told anyone exactly what Pastor Dale said to me, because of the shame it brought on me. As I wept bitterly remembering those words, I knew Father God was trying to restore my identity in Christ.

When he was done ministering to me, I no longer felt uncomfortable around him. I hugged him like he had thrown me a lifeline in a vast ocean. I realized that hurt comes in multiple layers, and healing would come in the same fashion. I was prepped and ready to criticize, and when Pastor Kent wept before me for things he did not do, I was met with a humility that broke those chains. God knew my heart was hard, and He knew how to reach me.

I realized that I had been looking for the opportunity to be offended. I considered it a careful precaution against being hurt again, which seemed legitimate and understandable. But I began to see that Kent had never done a thing to me, and yet, because he looked like the person that wrecked my life, I could not trust that he was not just like him. Ouch. My pre-conceived notion was a difficult pill to swallow. His love and humility revealed the hardness of my heart.

After I repented for shutting down my heart and asked God to give me a soft and pliable heart, I felt empowered with a new zeal bubbling on the inside. I was excited, and James was excited for me. He lovingly pushed me forward. Soon after the conversation with Pastor Kent, I started leading a women's group and helping on the ministry teams again. I felt fulfilled and excited to help others overcome difficulties and painful relationships, just as God had enabled me to do.

For the next several years, my freedom and passion led me to also work for an international network of churches, and my life became about ministry. We joyfully taught our children about the gifts of giving our time and energy to help others. James became a deacon, and once again, we were practically living at church.

James and I were thriving in our jobs. All three children, now nine, thirteen, and fifteen, were doing well. We were happy and satisfied. Life was still full of the normal struggles with juggling children, school, schedules, homework, and jobs, but we were making it work. We were a team.

Though our finances had remained a struggle for all of our married lives, we had grown and made sound decisions, and slowly, we saw the light and tried to remain joyful as God had clearly instructed us. It was sadly still the area where most disagreements came from. Not being able to do what others around us could do…well, let's say, that was a challenge.

Christmas that year was meager. James and I were recovering from the debt we created, but we were getting close to paying it off. Spending on anything not essential seemed like something other than wisdom. James was sick that Christmas with a sinus infection, making him a little cantankerous. Despite the minor upset, our big family Christmas meal was at McDonald's. We laughed and made the most of it. Maybe there was some complaining, but mostly because it was hard on the kids.

But we were confident this would be the last year of living so "close to the wire," as the saying goes. Next year would prove to be our best year yet financially. We tried to encourage the children with this positive perspective. They were old enough to understand, so they faked it as best they could.

As the holiday season ended, I was proud of our little family for how much we had grown in our ability to trust in the Lord when life looked a bit dismal. I saw each person trying to see beyond today to a brighter tomorrow. We were learning to make the hard decisions today so our future days would be lighter and easier to breathe. Also, we learned the essence of leaning into God, knowing that His "yoke is easy, and His burden is light" (Matthew 11:30 NIV).

Chapter Fourteen
BELIEVE

It doesn't matter what I feel or don't feel. It doesn't matter what I think or don't think. It doesn't matter what I see or don't see; I will trust HIM!
—Donna Bess

A brand-new year and we knew it was our year. We could feel it. We saw God's goodness in our personal lives, in our children, and at church. What could be more beautiful? These blank pages in the book called 1998 would be the best year ever. We made it through the previous tough holiday season with the call to spend money at every turn, and we held on to our limited budget. This was truly miraculous and could have only been done by the power of God. Our weakness was a testament to that truth.

The first week of the year, James called me from work. It was open enrollment for insurance. We had not had insurance for years because of an inability to pay for that privilege. We discussed what we should do, and we decided to add only James to the plan. Employees get the lowest rate; we could adjust to that and add the family next year. Besides, James had already had two sinus infections in three months, and we were getting doctor bills.

In late February, while I thanked God for his goodness, He gave me a word. "See your finances like cancer. You don't have the life you want but you still have life. Live it to its fullest." When James got home from work, I told him the word, and we talked about what "live it to its fullest" meant. We decided it had to do with joy. We had been so focused on getting out of debt that life had become debt focused. That was like cancer because it was stealing energy from us. We needed to focus on life. We needed to play more, laugh more, and live with more joy.

In the first week of April, we both got raises at work, which was just in time to start paying for the new insurance coverage on James. The excitement was palpable. At the rate we were going, all our debts could be paid off in less than a year. We dreamed of date nights and family excursions that could cost more than twenty dollars. Our marriage was growing, and now we were getting out of debt. The birds were singing, and the sun was out in our lives! What could be sweeter?

I have been a random journal writer all my Christian life. Some years only fill a few pages of a journal, and other years fill many journals. The only consistency I have had was to be inconsistent. A few years ago, I ripped all the pages from the many journals and filed them by year in one file box to keep track without carrying many mostly empty journals. 1998 was a meager year of journaling in a book. Unfortunately, I did most of it on a computer that was never backed up. UGH. Life!

I journaled in large letters sometime in the beginning months; I BELIEVE!!! It doesn't matter what I feel or don't feel. It doesn't matter what I think or don't think. It doesn't matter what I see or don't see. God has called me, and I will trust Him. I will step out in faith that He will guide, teach, protect, and bring it to pass. I BELIEVE! The fervent effectual prayer of the righteous man avails much. I will live from faith to faith to faith to faith…. You get the picture. I chose that God would remain King in my life no matter the cost. While there had been abundant testing to this point, the hope that sweeter days were on the horizon was alive in me.

There was some concern as James had vision problems in one eye, and the doctor told him again that it was a sinus issue. Since we now had insurance on James, I wanted something more done. I had no trained medical knowledge then, but I was not buying the idea that this sinus infection would improve when he took antibiotics and steroids. As soon as he was off the medication, the symptoms worsened again.

I made an appointment with another doctor on his insurance. That afternoon when we arrived for the appointment, we were seeing the physician's assistant. She was doing the normal well-visit examination, and I said, "I'm sorry, but if you don't plan on ordering a scan or something, can you just tell us so we can leave." She looked at me with the most incredulous look. I quickly apologized.

I explained that we had run up a bill at another doctor's office that kept giving antibiotics and steroids with no sustainable improvement. Her look changed to sympathy, and at the end of the visit, there was an order for an MRI the next morning. I was relieved that an answer was coming.

Chapter Fifteen
EVIL

"My hope is built on nothing less than Jesus' blood and righteousness. I dare not trust the sweetest frame but wholly lean on Jesus' name. On Christ the solid rock I stand, all other ground is sinking sand."
—Edward Mote

In the early hours of Monday, April 13, 1998, James and I were sitting in the Imaging Center of our local hospital. We were excited to be getting answers. James had now received treatment for sinus infection four or five times. As I mentioned, his vision problem in one eye only moderately improved with the treatment.

James was in and out of the MRI in forty-five minutes. They wanted him to sit in the waiting room until the doctor could look it over. So, we sat. And sat. Because we were expecting to be out of there quickly, we had not eaten breakfast and we were hungry. We sat for hours while many others came and left. Then we sat some more. After about four hours, James was getting hangry. I don't know if anyone knows what it is like to have a hangry spouse, but finding food for your own sanity becomes urgent.

I knocked on the door to see if the nurse could explain. She was apologetic and said she would check again with the doctor. After a few moments, she emerged from the locked door and, with a gentleness that told us she was sorry our day had been so hard, she said to us that

James needed to go down to the emergency room (ER) to be admitted and our doctor would meet us there to explain.

Can you imagine our shock? We had pretty much decided he would need sinus surgery, but that hardly seemed an emergency. Our knees were instantaneously weak, and our empty stomachs suddenly had an acid burn. We held each other's hands so tightly that my fingers felt numb, but unable to let go. We walked to the elevator silently, wondering how this would affect our life. Prayer was pinging around in my brain like a pinball machine—a new prayer with every thought. Let's just say that taking every thought captive felt like I would need anesthesia to stop this swirl. *Jesus, be with us. Jesus, help. Jesus, give wisdom. Be with the kids if this is bad; how will we manage? Jesus, you promise never to leave us or forsake us. Jesus, I'm counting on you. Be with us. We haven't eaten today. Food would be nice. Can someone bring us some food? Jesus!!*

After the admission process was completed, we were taken to a room in the ER. The cheerful nurse came in to start an IV and to draw blood. She gave no indication of what was going on. It seemed that everyone was waiting on this doctor. We had never met the doctor because we had seen the physician's assistant (PA) when we went to the office the previous day. So, we waited. And we waited some more. I was getting a quick education about what it means to be in the hospital. It can be summed up in four words. "Hurry up and wait." Hanger was taking on a new manifestation. All those around us seemed to have some foreknowledge about the gravity of this situation, but they were not sharing with us. It was completely unnerving.

People came in to do chest X-rays, draw more labs, and get an extensive history, and there was a sense of doom. I could feel it. James and I kept idle chit-chat going, mostly to manage the anxiety that was building from the unknown. We had been in the hospital for about seven hours without food or information.

After we had been in the ER for about an hour or so, a man dressed in scrubs poked his head in and asked if we believed in God. James said yes. The man said he would be praying for us. That was the straw that broke the camel's back. The nurse came in to check blood pressure, and James pronounced that not one more person would touch him before he found out why he was there. With understanding in her eyes, she turned and walked out the door.

A few moments later, the ER physician came in. He apologized for the confusion and explained that James had a doctor who had not met him and was reluctant to get involved in his case. So, the ER staff had been trying to arrange a few things. Then, with an intensity in his eyes that told us he would love not to be the person telling us what he was about to say, he took a deep breath. "Mr. Bess, I am afraid your scan showed that you have a sizable brain tumor. We are working now to get a neurosurgeon to see you; he should be here soon. When he comes, he will explain everything to you."

I felt like I needed oxygen to take a deep breath. We could not speak and could barely breathe. *Brain tumor?* A word kept circulating in the recesses of my mind, but I couldn't focus on it. *Believe!* I'm sure the gentle whisper was my faithful Father, but all I could focus on was *brain tumor, brain tumor, brain tumor,* and then another whisper in my thoughts, *Believe.*

After a moment, the doctor was gone. We were alone. We didn't cry. I think we were in shock. Suddenly all the solemn looks and that guy's offer to pray for us made sense. Or did it? We were in the emergency room. I didn't imagine brain tumors were that unusual. I heard a quiet voice in my spirit, *Don't think, Donna. Just believe.* I finally rallied myself, passed the desperate thoughts, and was back on solid ground. I will trust God. He had this! I reminded James of the words I recently got from the Lord. He is here, I said. He has gone before us to prepare us. We need to hold on to Him with all we have in us.

About an hour or so later, the long-awaited neurosurgeon came in and took a seat. This was a man used to hard conversations. He smiled and looked confident. He said that James would be going to surgery in the morning. My brain was screaming, *What are you saying?* but no sound from my mouth. My thoughts continued, *Tomorrow morning? Is this that big of an emergency? Is James going to die?* A whisper came to my thoughts once again, *believe.* Then the neurosurgeon explained that based on the scan, he was pretty sure it was the worst kind of brain cancer, but he would not be sure until the biopsy results came back, which would be three to four days. As he left, he ordered food to be brought to us. Funny, we were no longer hungry.

He asked if we had any questions. My thoughts were a bit angry and sarcastic. *Questions? How do I breathe again? You guys leave us hanging for about eight hours without information, and when all of our strength and stamina are gone, you hit us between the eyes? I have a question. What the heck?* But again, my angry questions were only in my head, and no voice came with them. Between the anger and terror, I struggled to be a strength for James. I couldn't show my anger because I was working hard to keep him calm. But truthfully, we were a mess for a little time before we could even think of legitimate questions. By then, the surgeon was gone, and we would have to ask them tomorrow. For now, we just needed to tell our family we were not coming home tonight.

Once those details were taken care of, I needed to speak life in this dark place. I needed it for myself and James. We were badly shaken. All of our life was finally going right, and now this. *What now, Lord?*

The old hymn comforted my soul. "My hope is built on nothing less than Jesus' blood and righteousness. I dare not trust the sweetest frame but wholly lean on Jesus' name. On Christ the solid rock I stand, all other ground is sinking sand." I reminded James and myself that we could make this another testimony of God's power, but we must cling to Jesus! It will be a battle, but it is the Lord's to win. All we had to do was trust Him!

Chapter Sixteen
THE GOD WHO SEES ME

When I am afraid, I put my trust in you. In God, whose word I praise—in God I trust and am not afraid.
—Psalm 56:3–4 NIV

The next morning, we were awakened very early; James signed papers absolving the hospital of any complications. His head was shaved, and a light sedative was given. Finally, he was taken to the operating room (OR). As we said our goodbyes, we both had tears of terror behind our words of confident pronouncement that God has this in His hands. We wanted to declare the truth, and we did. Our souls were terrified children trying to hide in our Father's lap. We were afraid of what might be found. We told God we were terrified but would trust Him with the outcome. We knew this journey would not be for the faint-hearted, and we were determined to rise to the challenge.

The next several hours are lost to me. I don't know where I went or with whom I might have been. I am completely blank. I can assume that I sat in the surgery waiting room because that is where everyone waits, but I don't remember that experience. It was as if I was asleep with James.

My next memory is seeing James in recovery. He looked swollen but peaceful, still asleep from the sedation, and his head wrapped with a gauze turban. The surgeon came in to check on him and told me the surgery went very well. He had "evacuated the tumor and left chemo wafers in the void." In layman's terms, he took out the tumor and put small wafers coated with chemo in the hole that was left. I asked if he had gotten all the cancer. It seemed like such a smart question to ask. He replied, "I hope so, but we will know more when the biopsy results come back in four to five days."

Though his answer offered hope, his face was stoic and not a look of confidence, reminiscent of the responses we received the previous day in the ER. He knows what is going on. It was etched on his face, but he was unwilling to say. I was sure of it. I think hospital people are skilled at trying to protect you, but I wonder if they don't just make it worse. For me, I wanted to know. It was the "not knowing" that was torture. He said we wouldn't know much until James woke up and the biopsy results returned.

When James woke in his still groggy state, he smiled, and his first words to me were, "I can see normal again." Only then did I consider how awful it must have been for him to see double out of one eye for a few months. I now had a few questions for the doctor who repeatedly treated him for a sinus infection. Clearly, he had misdiagnosed James. But God followed that thought with a great revelation.

April 1, just twelve days earlier, was the first day James had health insurance coverage for the first time in many years. God went before us and blinded that doctor to the truth. Had the diagnosis come before…ugh, I didn't even want to go down that road. Suddenly I was filled with gratitude. God had gone before us, which meant He was still going before us. I needed to cling to that truth like a dying man in the desert would savor a glass of water. I knew God was calling us to fix our eyes on Him. This verse nearly became my mantra as I warred the emotions that tried to overtake my thoughts. "And let us run with perseverance the race marked out for us, fixing our eyes on Jesus, the pioneer and perfecter of faith" (Hebrews 12:1b and 2a NIV).

If ever I doubted anything, now was the time to defeat doubt and "Believe!" I could sense that this storm was going to be ugly. Matthew 8:24, however, tells us that a furious storm raged on the lake that swept over the boat, but Jesus was sleeping. *Oh, Lord, build my faith!* As if that wasn't exactly what He was doing.

The rest of the week was about healing and preparing for the next thing. Enough had been said that we were hoping for the best but preparing for the worst. Or so we thought. When Friday came, and the biopsy results were back, we thought we were ready, but no, we were not.

James and I were sitting and chatting when the surgeon came in. His solemn, no-nonsense face was firmly planted. His jaw set. He looked a little like one preparing for battle. He said, "The biopsy results are in, and they are as I expected. You have grade 4 Glioblastoma Multiforme." I was scrambling in my mind to make sense of those words. His tone told me it was bad, but how bad?

I asked the most obvious. "There are things that you can do for this cancer. Right?"

He responded, "Well, we can do gamma knife, chemo, and radiation."

Okay, again…what the heck? I know he has to understand what I am searching for. I asked, "So these things can overcome this cancer?"

He responded, "There is hope that the combination of drugs will effectively reduce the tumor."

What? This man was not speaking my language. I tried again, "So he will be…okay?"

With exasperation that he could no longer hide, he spouted like a hose under pressure, "I'm telling you…your husband will be dead within six months. Sorry." He turned and walked out the door.

When the door opened, I became aware of our three children standing on the other side of that door with Aunt Diann, waiting to see their father. As the door shut, I placed my hand on his chest, willed every ounce of control into him, and whispered to James, "The kids are here. I'm okay. Are you okay?" Trying desperately to hold the torrent of tears that were screaming for release, I asked, "Can you wait to deal with this until the kids leave?"

With a clenched jaw, he nodded yes.

I opened the door and let them in. They came in filled with sunshine and questions. We needed more time to be ready to answer. I caught Diann's eye and mouthed, "Take them out. I'll explain later." She quickly caught on and suggested ice cream with a calm confidence that contradicted her concern and questions. Our children seemed oblivious to the terror that had just stepped into their innocent lives. They were all in agreement with ice cream and left excitedly.

When the door closed, our tear ducts opened fully to allow all the pent-up emotions of the week to purge. I laid my head on his chest, and we sobbed tears of fear, relief that the beast had a name, anxiety about how we would help our children through this, and most importantly, how we would deal with such an uncertain future. We were certainly in deep water, and the water fell at the level of my nose. Less than "SIX MONTHS?" How can the doctor say less than six months with such conviction? After the long torrent of tears brought some release, my confession and resolve became that Jesus is Lord, and I can trust that He paid for this on the cross. It will all be okay, even if I don't know how. I must believe it.

I BELIEVE!!! It doesn't matter what I feel or don't feel. It doesn't matter what I think or don't think. It doesn't matter what I see or don't see. God has called me, and I will trust Him. We discussed what Jesus would have us do and how we needed to tell the children. We prayed for wisdom.

The next day we left the hospital and headed home to our very different life. We had gained a new perspective. "Teach us to number our days, that we may gain a heart of wisdom" (Psalm 90:12 NIV). God reminded me of this word. *See your finances like cancer. You don't have the life you want, but you still have life. Live it to its fullest.*

God reminded us of the importance of fixing our eyes on Him alone. Next, we needed to figure out how to communicate that to the children. I didn't know how because the cancer was "noise" so loud that it was hard to block it out and fix my eyes on Jesus. I knew I had to, and more importantly, I would have to help my sweet children do the same. I whispered, "I need you now, Lord."

Once we were home, we gathered in the family room. I was the one who spoke. James was struggling a bit. Ha. I say that as if I was not battling my emotions. The struggle was so real, but the desire to be what my children needed most was far more real. I prayed even as we took our seats. James sat next to me as I laid out the diagnosis. I did not tell them the doctor's prognosis, because I believed that to be a lie from the devil.

I read two verses: "A person's days are determined; you have decreed the number of his months and have set limits he cannot exceed" (Job 14:5 NIV), and "Your eyes saw my unformed body; all the days ordained for me were written in your book before one of them came to be" (Psalm 139:16 NIV).

I explained that God alone knows the number of our days. Doctors are not God, so we would move forward listening to medical advice from doctors, but we would know that God has a plan we would want to partner with.

Our children sat in numbness that I understood all too well for a few moments. There were many questions, but only a few, which were the hardest, remained in my memory. "Will Dad be here when I graduate high school?" "Will Dad be able to walk me down the aisle when I get married?" "What will happen to us if Dad dies?" There was a lot of fear and anxiety circulating in the room, but we all did our best.

As our conversation was wrapping up, I prayed and reminded each of us that the choice to stay positive would be hard and constant as we moved forward, but that positivity would be our stance. We talked about the reality that none of us is guaranteed tomorrow. It was up to us to live our best lives daily with hope and love.

When the conversation was over, and the questions were answered to the best of our ability, we all went to our rooms. Some of us went in our own spaces to cry, but we all needed time to process. However, during the next several weeks, cancer became our new norm with daily radiation treatments and doctor visits galore.

The testing of our commitment started early and came in some of the most unsuspected ways. Our church family began to bring in meals.

There were many questions and promises to pray for us. But some had done some research and wanted to regale me with their knowledge. Those who needed to tell me the likely bad outcome predicted by man's evidence wanted to protect me from being disappointed. Several intimated that the outcome was sure and bleak, and my belief that he would be healed was denial. Although these words initially hurt, I learned to guard the promise that God had given me. It was like when Jesus said to Peter, "Get behind me, Satan! You are a stumbling block to me; you do not consider God's concerns merely human concerns." The devil will use others to try to take my hope if I let them.

Let me end this section with this statement: If someone has been given an unfortunate diagnosis and wants to discuss it, then, by all means, share whatever God leads you to share. But otherwise, be kind or be quiet. Mostly, they need a friend to listen to them and not give advice. It is a tough road. I'm reminded of the story of Pooh and Piglet.

> "Today was a Difficult Day," said Pooh. There was a pause. "Do you want to talk about it?" asked Piglet. "No," said Pooh after a bit. "No, I don't think I do." "That's okay," said Piglet, and he came and sat beside his friend. "What are you doing?" asked Pooh. "Nothing, really," said Piglet. "Only I know what Difficult Days are like. I quite often don't feel like talking about it on my Difficult Days either." "But goodness," continued Piglet, "Difficult Days are so much easier when you know you've got someone there for you. And I'll always be here for you, Pooh." And as Pooh sat there, working through in his head his Difficult Day, while the solid, reliable Piglet sat next to him quietly, swinging his little legs…he thought that his best friend had never been more right.

The truth was, because we were facing many decisions about chemotherapy and radiation, I had already searched the internet and was familiar with all the negative reports. I didn't want to hear ANY negative pronouncements from my friends and family. I needed them to believe with me.

When James' radiation treatments were half completed, I had done all the research I could and shared my findings with James. He decided to finish radiation. However, the evidence for chemo was questionable at best. After discussing all I could learn about chemo, James and I decided not to do chemotherapy. The evidence did not favor those with primary brain cancer at the time. Other than that decision, we left the rest to the doctor overseeing his care. We understood that less than one percent lived past six months and nobody past eighteen months. The doctors made that very clear, as did the research. We had to fight to keep faith in this journey. I cried a lot in those initial days as I wrestled with doubt. The following verse became my confession. "Jesus replied, 'Truly I tell you, if you have faith and do not doubt, not only can you do what was done to the fig tree, but also you can say to this mountain, "Go, throw yourself into the sea,"' and it will be done'" (Matthew 21:21 NIV). His Word is final, the cancer must be cast into the sea. It is defeated. No doubt!

Another test came with transportation. James had been driving a company car. With the diagnosis of brain cancer, their insurance would no longer cover him. The car had to go back. We only owned one car, and it was on its last leg. All the driving necessary for doctor visits and my job would not work with our current vehicle. The mechanics didn't want to fix it; they said it was beyond hope and only good for scrap.

We missed church that Sunday because we didn't have transportation to church, but we heard an offering was taken up. In a church of only two hundred people (including families with children) and many in similar financial situations to ours, I didn't have much hope that a car would come from those precious people, but I knew God would provide from somewhere.

God provided the miracle we needed for transportation. One story that touched me deeply was from a woman in our church that felt led to put $1,000 toward a vehicle that would be needed. He didn't tell her by whom or when the need would come up. She kept the money aside for over a year—even through a move to another state. She trusted God and waited for a need to come up. Wow!

Like Hagar said in Genesis 16, God is a God who sees. He saw me and was making a way "a long time ago." Somehow, I knew He was preparing us. He had gone before us to make a way. We could trust Him. I felt a stirring in my soul as a gentle whisper. "Keep your eyes fixed on Me. I make the roadway in the wilderness, and I am faithful. I will make something beautiful from all this." We didn't have to understand it or see it, we just had to trust in the One who would accomplish it if we just stayed fixed on Him. God is greater than anything in our circumstances.

Within one week, we received a magnificent gift of a beautiful red Dodge caravan. It was used but in great condition and a humongous blessing! My faith increased. I was living out the following promise: "The Lord himself goes before you and will be with you; he will never leave you nor forsake you. Do not be afraid; do not be discouraged" (Deuteronomy 31:8 NIV). God had indeed gone before us. The gift of that car was one that proved that He saw my need before I was born, and He had already made provision. That gift helped me cling to Him. I felt testing was coming, and I hoped I could remain strong in His promise. I asked that Jesus pray for me that my faith would not fail.

Chapter Seventeen
MERCY AND GRACE FIND ME

Grace, mercy, and peace from God the Father and from Jesus Christ, the Father's Son, will be with us in truth and love.
—2 John 1:3 NIV

For the first eighteen months beating the odds progressed rather well. Oh, believe me, there were plenty of bumps, but the beast dwelling in my husband's head was not winning. Our lives progressed along with those bumps as we stood on truth and saw the miracles of God. James became the poster child in the neurology department. Because he was walking free of assistive devices and had "normal cognition" well past their expected time frame, they analyzed and prodded to determine how this was possible and why the tumor stopped growing. It was such a beautiful testimony of God's goodness. He had a Grade 4 Glioblastoma Multiforme brain tumor. This diagnosis is terminal. Nobody has lived past eighteen months. His tumor didn't shrink, but it also didn't grow. The very fact that James was eighteen months into this diagnosis pointed to the miracle he was living. Only God could get the glory!

When we went for regular checkups every few months, the doctor would sometimes take James around and introduce him to staff or even an occasional patient as proof that there is always room for optimism. We marveled at the power of God when given a chance, in hopes those patients that needed to believe in the possibility of life would see it was a far higher power than the staff in this office and the medications in James' body. We delighted in the magnificence of God. He was showing off His power to heal. Despite the constant testing, we stayed strong. People worldwide were praying for James to be healed and for our family to remain strong in the Lord and be encouraged. We felt their prayers and encouragement. Even though it was so hard, I counted it a privilege to walk out this healing testimony. I met each day with truth and a decision that Christ would rule and reign in this home, and cancer would die. He was with us. We were not battling this alone because His grace and mercy was evident everywhere we turned.

At this time, I felt I needed to pursue an education. Although I loved working in ministry, it was a work of passion rather than one that would financially provide for our family. James and I prayed about it and believed it was the right time for me to make the leap. Also, it was verified and supported by the leadership in our church.

Twenty-one months after James was given a terminal diagnosis with less than a six month to live prognosis, I started nursing school. I'm not going to lie; starting school at forty was a bit of a challenge. It was enlightening, especially when my peers were only three to ten years older than my children. However, I thrived in that world. Though I was like a mother to most, and I was happy to be there for them, in my mind, I was just another student. In that environment, one hundred percent focus is required to succeed. Though you may have a job, family, and other responsibilities, there is hardly room to consider them when you are in the midst of learning. My education turned out to be my saving grace. I was forced to turn off the cares of my personal world (mostly) and focus on learning the tools and information that would someday save someone else's life.

At orientation on the first day of the nursing program, seventy-five students sat shoulder to shoulder, anxious and excited about the new venture. We had one thing in common; we were starting a life-changing journey. They told us to "look to your right and your left. Only one of you will be standing on graduation day."

I smiled and proclaimed, "Geez, I am so sorry you guys aren't going to make it because I will be standing at graduation." We all laughed.

About that time, the instructors said, "Go home, kiss your kids, your husbands, and your family goodbye. Tell them you will see them again when you finish school."

Wow, these people were serious. It was terrifying to sit in that room. However, the logic of their madness worked for me. From that day forward, I was focused. I would pass, no doubt about it.

About three months after Abba Father assured me that school was the right thing at the right time, the testing at home mounted to a whole other level. James suddenly developed a mild right extremity leg, arm, and hand weakness. This development changed our lives forever. Though it minimally affected his activities of daily living, the job that meant everything to James had to be discontinued. The owner decided it was too dangerous for James to be on construction job sites, so they let him go.

James was distraught by losing his job, and while he respected his boss and understood it was necessary, I could tell the news was a severe blow to him mentally. Unfortunately, it resulted in an immediate decline in his coping ability. He was more easily angered, and tensions at home began to increase. I encouraged him to look for a job close to home that he could get to with his scooter.

Fortunately, he landed a job as a host at a local restaurant only a half mile from home. It was wonderful for him to work with people, and he enjoyed his time there. This also helped some to restore his independence and bring more peace back into our home. It also gave him stories to share about his workday. It was wonderfully helpful, and I realized his ability to work was paramount to our success on this journey.

I also recognized that as the cancer's challenges increased, it resulted in an equivocal increase in James' anger. The greater his loss of independence, the greater his rage. It scared me. After thinking about our finances and concerns for our home life, I thought it best to quit school when the semester ended.

I can't say I prayed about it, but I was needed at home much more than I could be present. I talked with James, and he was fine with it. He would be happy that I would be around more to attend to his every need, and I could continue my job with the church, which had abundant flexibility. I could go to school at another time. God would provide for our finances in another way.

The next afternoon, I was at school and was going to meet with one of my professors, most of whom were about my age, for lunch. As I was waiting for this professor to finish up a meeting with another one of her students, I was leaning against the wall in the hallway reading my notes. I felt someone approaching me. I looked up, and a sea of students were surrounding me as they waited to enter a nearby classroom. To the left, there was a well-groomed black woman, with a suit and a scarf, on the shorter side and a little chunky, walking toward me, and it was as if the sea of students were parting for her to come. I didn't recognize her. I could feel her presence coming closer. She smiled as she came closer. She said, "You look so nice in that green shirt."

I replied, "Thank you," thinking it was so faded.

She then asked, "What are you going to school for?"

I said, "Nursing."

She responded, "You will be so good at that. Keep it up." Then she walked away.

I admit I might have rolled my eyes. Was it the green shirt that clued her into my success in nursing? Did she see me in green scrubs? I didn't know, but I chalked it up as weird and returned to my notes.

My professor emerged from her office a few moments later. She asked if I was ready for lunch. I laughed, "Yes, and I have a story for you." We went to the cafeteria, got our lunch, and went outside to eat. We sat on the warm sunny patio with a beautiful garden area surrounding the courtyard. It always refreshed my soul to eat lunch out in the beautiful afternoon garden.

I told her that this very well-groomed, professionally dressed black woman that was medium height, a little chunky, with short hair walked up to me. I explained how I had an awareness before she got near me, as if the students were making a path for her straight to me. I explained what she said and then admitted that I thought it was weird how she just said her piece and walked away. My professor responded, "Interesting; well, you would be good at nursing, and I do wish you wouldn't quit."

I didn't have to explain my life to her. She was a professor of psychology, and when I had her class the previous semester, I shared all kinds of stories from my personal life. As we became friends, she heard even more. So, I just smiled and said, "I must do what I must do. Also, I can't create more debt to go to school. We have so much now." She nodded in understanding, and the conversation changed course.

We finished lunch, and I went to an isolated place to study alone on the other side of the campus. I liked to go upstairs in the student services building, particularly at this time of day, when it was empty on the second floor. After I went to the restroom there, I was standing at the sink washing my hands, and the same woman who commented on my green shirt on the other side of campus came into the bathroom and walked up to the wall of sinks in front of a long mirror. Making eye contact with me in the mirror, she said, "You will face many obstacles, and it will be hard, but stay the course. You will be good at nursing, so don't quit." She then turned and walked away. Immediately it hit me that she was in this isolated place to do what? She didn't go to the bathroom. She didn't wash her hands. I ran to the door with my hands still dripping with water and opened the door and…she was gone!

Chapter Eighteen
MY ANGEL

*For he will command his angels concerning you
to guard you in all your ways.
—Psalm 91:11 NIV*

As I stood in this nearly empty building on campus, I listened for the sound of footsteps. There were none. I called out, "Ma'am?" There was no answer. It was clear that I was alone, and it gave me goosebumps on my whole body. I went back and sat down in the quiet. In my spirit, I knew she was an angel. "Lord, it seems you are trying to get the message to me to stay in school. I don't see a way, but I will obey." I can't say I understood how it would happen because it seemed impossible to pull off, but I trusted that my faithful Father told me to continue and that He would move on my behalf.

After this experience, I reflected on another experience I had blown off the night before. Because our finances were in such bad shape, I called to stop payment to a prepaid contract account that we had started for a funeral plan over a year previously. We thought it would help protect the children from that burden when we passed. However, we signed a contract, so I thought there might be a fight.

I explained that our financial situation had changed, and I could no longer make the payments. I was now in school and making significantly less money. Then very weirdly, she asked me what I was going to school for. I told her about nursing. She said, "Oh, that is so good. You will make a great nurse." I said thank you and asked if that meant she would stop the contract. She said, "Yes, no problem. You will not be billed further. Have a great day." I hung up the phone and told James about the conversation, and we laughed. We laughed about how easy God had made it to get out of the contract. It was definitely a bizarre comment from a stranger on the other end of the phone!

But sitting there after I met the angel woman two different times in two completely random ways, who disappeared seconds after she spoke to me? I felt sure. The God of the Universe is interested in me staying the course; He sent me my angel twice! Or maybe even three times. The one thing I was convinced of was that I would be making a mistake if I quit.

I called James to tell him about the encounter. I wasn't sure what he would say as he wanted me to quit and return to work. But, to my shock, he said, "I tell you what, Donna, if you decide to quit school, don't come home because I think the house will be struck by lightning." And so it was; I continued in school thanks to my complete assurance that my Heavenly Father would carry me and my sweet children under His wings to see this thing through.

Chapter Nineteen
ADAPT AND OVERCOME

Adaptation requires a willingness to bend.
If you refuse to turn, neither can you overcome.
Overcoming is a choice we must pursue.
—Donna Bess

Depression settling into James' heart, combined with appetite-inducing medications, was driving James into a life of inactivity, resulting in increased weight and decreased desire to move. These issues led to reduced speed at work, and only six to seven months after he started, they could no longer allow him to continue. That blow landed him on the recliner in front of the television. It scared me because he was becoming increasingly depressed and exponentially angry. Peace in our home seemed like a thing of the past. Desperate for anything that would give him a sense of purpose, I suggested volunteer work. I reminded him of Psalm 118:17 NIV, "I will not die but live, and will proclaim what the Lord has done." It is gratitude that brings healing.

One day when we were at the hospital for a procedure, I recommended that he volunteer there. It took some pleading, but he relented and applied. They hired him to deliver mail, flowers, and other items to patient rooms which he could do on an electric scooter. For several months, he took the medical transport van from home to the hospital and back home each day he worked.

I prayed it would continue because the more he stayed home, the worse it was for the kids. I was now tied up at school five days a week, and I didn't have the freedom to stop what I was doing to manage a problem. With their ages thirteen, sixteen, and nineteen, I felt a bit more secure not being available as much, but it was hard on my heart.

Regrettably, James sometimes waited several long hours past his scheduled pick-up time for the transport van to arrive for his trip home. These hours of feeling helpless only elevated his exasperation and amplified his loss of independence. This eventually led to increased annoyance, and then fury overtook his commitment to help others.

Thankfully, as if I could foresee the potential nightmare coming to take residence in our home, I sought counseling right after James lost his job at the restaurant. Nelson was a professional counselor that attended our church, so he was well acquainted with our situation. The first day I saw him, he asked what brought me in. I told him I needed to navigate a minefield and make sure my children came out on the other side as whole, well-adjusted citizens of the Kingdom of God. With so many responsibilities weighing on me, I wasn't always attuned to what was needed, especially concerning the children. I was very hesitant with so many financial issues, but I went anyway, and he graciously worked with our finances. God is always working!

During my first session with the counselor, Nelson had me questioning if I had heard God. He instructed me to get a cell phone. In the year 2000, only people with money considered such a luxury. I had a pager, and it seemed adequate. However, sometimes twenty or thirty minutes could go by before I had access to a pay phone, and Nelson said my children needed to know they could get ahold of me at a moment's notice for them to feel safe. That was all I needed to convince me. Again, I knew God would provide for that cell phone. The cell phone helped bring me peace as well. Some other items Nelson recommended that I implemented were as follows:

- Weekly family meetings with only myself and the children. James was excluded. They needed the freedom to speak their hearts without fear of repercussions.

- Take one child out for ice cream or something each week so they would have time alone with me. This venture seemed harder on our meager budget and my extremely stretched time. However, I did it. It proved to be a valuable time to learn what they would not say in front of their siblings. We had some deep and meaningful conversations in those settings.

- Finally, he recommended I find each child an adult mentor they could talk freely to. This adult needed to be someone I trusted enough to not need to know what he or she and one of my children talked about. The only exception would be if the situation was potentially catastrophic, and then I would need to know immediately, like if one of them wanted to run away.

I followed through on all his advice. My son maintains that relationship even to this day. That man is the father Jarred had been missing.

When James decided he would not suffer the imposition of medical transport one more time, he quickly descended into the dark world of resentment and despair. During a family discussion with the children in my bedroom, they asked me if I would consider divorcing him. Can I just be honest? This request broke my heart, and not for the reason you might think. It was terrible that his children would want to get him out of their lives. But worse for me was the fear that the image of their earthly father was tainting their idea of their Heavenly Father. It is a common belief that children first develop their perspective of God from their earthly fathers. I was frightened by what they may perceive about their Heavenly Father if that belief was true.

But I also understood that the pain was so great they wanted it to stop by any means possible, even if it was a divorce. I was grateful I had listened to Nelson and set up weekly family meetings that included just myself and the three children. He, indeed, had the wisdom of the Lord. Because, as hard as it was to hear that our children would prefer a divorce, how much greater their pain would be to feel those feelings and be afraid to tell me. I believed that them speaking about their misery helped them release at least a small portion of it. I clung to a perspective of hope and thanked God for the hope He gave me.

I explained to our kids that we made a vow to marry in sickness and in health. They argued that it was not a sickness that made him this way. "He laughs and jokes at church and acts fine when out with others. He only acts this way when he is alone with us." Although James' behavior was not news to me, I had not realized the kids had been so observant. It was overwhelming for me to see their pain. I told them it was more complicated than they knew, and we would all have to lean harder on the Lord for our peace and joy. I shared that God is a good Father, and He loves each of us. I went on to say that we must trust that He has a plan for all of us in this journey, including for their dad. I ended our discussion with prayer, as always. "Father, hear your children. We are tired of living in this angry environment. Please do what only You can do, making roadways in this wilderness and rivers in this desert to bring us relief in our home."

I admit, sometimes my prayers were prayed in full-fledged doubt. I realized that four of the five of us living in our home wanted peace. But the one who wanted independence, who could not be content without it, was too angry to seek God. I began to pray for water for our thirsty souls. The kids and I needed a path through; we needed our thirst quenched in this dry place.

As my discussion with the kids wrapped up, I had mixed feelings of brokenness and gratitude. Our time together proved that my children knew they were loved and protected, and I would do anything to keep it that way. God indeed ordered those steps for His protection over us. It helped us survive the continued crisis of our home and protected us in ways I was yet to understand.

Frankly, despite the good that God was doing in James' health, we were all tired. James seemed incapable of gleaning from the word that

God spoke before we began this journey, even though I would remind him. "You don't have the life you want but still have life. Live it to its fullest." He wanted independence, and nothing short of that was acceptable. Instead, he dwelt in anger and bitterness.

I learned that breathing in your body is different from being alive. As the cancer journey lengthened, James grew increasingly weary and angry as his limitations increased. I then began to struggle with anger and fear, especially related to how he was treating our children. I often repented for not seeing that God loved my children more than I ever could. But it was so hard for me to understand why my prayers were seemingly making no difference. I prayed regularly for James to soften and see the damage he was causing in our home because of his inability to lay selfish issues down. This way was probably not the greatest way to pray, but it was evidence of where my heart was.

When I could quiet my emotions and be with the Lord, my heart was refilled with the sustaining words through verses He gave me during this season.

> "Be strong and courageous. Do not be afraid or terrified because of them, for the LORD your God goes with you; he will never leave you nor forsake you" (Deuteronomy 31:6 NIV).

> "For I know the plans I have for you," declares the LORD, "plans to prosper you and not to harm you, plans to give you hope and a future" (Jeremiah 29:11 NIV).

Counseling helped me with raising the children in our anger-filled environment. However, because my focus during those sessions was on the kids, I needed additional help. I went to a brain tumor support group. James would not go with me, and he was angry because of my request for us to go together. I, however, was desperate to understand what was happening to James. I needed to find a way to help him.

That first night at the brain tumor support group was my last. The wind in my sails was sucked dry, and I crashed against the shore of reality. There was a neuropsychologist speaking that night. When he was done, I had the opportunity to ask questions privately. I told him what I saw happening with James. This neuropsychologist asked me many additional questions during the next ten minutes. Then with the seriousness of a man telling me I was about to die, he pronounced this verdict.

"This brain tumor is sort of like an amputated leg. Life will never look the same. You may walk with a limp or perhaps not walk at all. You can't do the things you used to do. But you can learn to do other things and enjoy them." (*This sounded like the word God gave me before this all started about not having the life you want, but having life. Live it to its fullest.*) "However, your husband was an alcoholic that quit alcohol and turned his addictive behavior to work. He has found his identity in being a workaholic. Now he cannot hold a job that fills that need, and he is stuck at home while his wife and children are out living their lives. He is mad, and because he has had a history of anger issues already, it will be expressed in anger toward those who have what he wants. Freedom. Until he gets that, I am sorry to say, it will not be an easy road for you or your children."

I wanted to rebuke the lie. I wanted to believe Jesus would alter our course. But somewhere in the depths of my heart, I knew that this doctor was right. It certainly seemed like it had been true so far. I cried out to God for mercy and cried out in frustration as well. With our lives going from difficult to impossible, I began to feel pressed and lost. A lack of hope led me into an angry prison. I found myself with such contemptible anger, which manifested in distance rather than outrage. I had no more words. I had talked, prayed, and even tried to manipulate James into getting help. But he declined in no uncertain terms. My soul felt dark, and I marched forward in the shadows daily. People at church prayed without ceasing for healing and for the natural struggles that illness brings to a home.

The thing is, at church, he was nice, controlled, and never angry. He laughed and joked easily, as the children had already pointed out. It appeared like he was content and a happy cancer patient walking in the sunshine. It was only at home that his demons came out. Unfortunately, it wasn't easy to avoid taking his behavior personally.

Although all of us were affected, Jarred seemed to be impacted the most. He remained locked in a battle against his father. Most of James' anger was first exhibited towards me. I would do anything to diffuse it, so it didn't spread to the children. But Jarred became my sixteen-year-old protector (making his own decision, but it wasn't one I liked). He could not allow his father to speak to me the way that he did. They locked horns regularly in their quest for dominance. Jarred would scream at James, "Do not speak to her that way. She is doing everything to help this family. You don't have a right to treat her like that."

James would scream at Jarred, "You are not the parent, and you cannot speak to me like that." It was always downhill from there.

The fury from their war of words spread like fire through the house, consuming everything in its wake. No matter how often I tried to get Jarred to leave it alone and allow me, "the parent," to handle his father, Jarred did not have it within him to tolerate the injustice. Anger was taking over my home, burning furiously. As much as I wanted to deny it, the devil seemed to be winning the battle. Henry Cloud said, "Anger is frustration at the fact that we are not God and do not have control over reality."[3] Truer words were never spoken. We had no control over anything, and we were so angry and hurt.

Chapter Twenty
THE DAY THE
WORLD STOOD STILL

We say we fear the unknown. But it is instead the vain imagination about the unknown that drives fear.
—*Donna Bess*

One particular day started like any other day in nursing school. Each day was filled with some form of angst. A pop quiz, a big test, or doing a new skill. As always, we were met with high expectations. This particular day was also the first of my surgical rotation. Our instructors had warned us that surgeons love to question nursing students about their knowledge of the surgery they are watching. "Make sure," they said, "you have read your book regarding the surgery you will be observing so you know what to expect, and so you don't sound like you don't have a clue about what is happening."

With that warning, I was as ready as I could be for this big day. I had studied, and I was now dressed in my sterile personal protective equipment, which included a mask, a hair cover, a gown covering, as well as scrubs, gloves, and shoe covers. I walked into the operating room (OR) behind the registered nurse who I would be observing.

Within a few moments, all the surgical team had prepared their portion of the room, the patient was prepared, and we waited for the surgeon. Easy banter went back and forth among the staff of the OR as they checked and double checked their responsibilities to have the room and supplies prepared. The patient lay waiting in the middle of the room making some light conversations with me as I seemed to be the only one not busy.

At 8:30 a.m., we had finished with the standard three-minute hand scrub, and the surgeon walked into the sterile white room. He stepped in and was met with people standing to assist him with shoe covers, a sterile gown, and his psychedelic cap already in place. Facing the nurse, the surgeon held up his hands for her to don his sterile gloves and turned to speak with the patient about what surgery they will perform and asks if he has any questions. He did not. He was ready to sleep and wake up on the other side of this operation.

The patient was asleep within seconds, and the surgeon was ready to begin. I had just experienced a precision mastered by repetition of preparing a patient and a room for surgery. I noticed the surgeon looking over the counters that are well outside the sterile field. I found myself wondering what he was possibly looking for over there. Everything he needed was within his immediate radius because the five other staff in the room had checked and double-checked. As his gaze made it around, he asked where the radio was, and the nurse yelled for someone outside the OR to bring in the radio.

I discovered music in the OR is common. Many surgeons prefer to have music playing as it assists them in conducting their mastery of the operation being performed. Expecting some fine classical music, which is probably what I would listen to if I was a surgeon, the station suddenly screams out with heavy metal music I could never have anticipated. The surgery started, everyone seemed to settle into a rhythm. I, on the other hand, was praying this surgery would not take long as the music was already fraying my nerves.

The masterful surgical concerto had begun, and the nurse was describing to me what was happening. Then, suddenly, at 8:47 a.m., a nurse came running into the room with a white face yelling, "Let me change your station." With all eyes on her, most everyone instinctively knew something bad was happening. On the other hand, I was just relieved that the wretched music was being changed. I had no idea that it was a breach of protocol for anyone to come into the OR once surgery had started, except for an emergency. But with all eyes staring, I turned to look at her while she turned the dial on this miniature "ghetto-blaster." She quickly turned from the radio and announced, "A plane just hit one of the twin towers of the World Trade Center."

A hush fell over the room. The surgeon was the first to break the silence with a statement that felt almost humorous to me. He said, "My dad is heading to his bomb shelter. He has been predicting this attack for a long while." A few others added to the conversation. I silently felt an incredulous gasp of pity rise in my heart for the poor souls living in such fear. Then silence again took over the room as everyone was glued to the news reports from the radio. Surgery continued, and the room had a sense of normalcy. I assumed it was an accident, and while silently grieving for the families that would lose a loved one today, I still felt my world intact. But with surgery resumed as normal, the radio broke in with thoughts about what had happened. Some immediately suggested it was a terrorist attack.

My first thoughts were: *A TERRORIST attack? What would make one plane flying into one tower a terrorist attack?* The surgeon's statement about his dad was now repeated in my head. Am I naive? *He predicted something like this would happen." PREDICTED? Why would someone expect that?* I felt I was a clueless wonder in the room as others nodded in understanding. I wondered if they nodded in agreement because they would not disagree with the surgeon or if I was the only uninformed person in the room. As I stood in disbelief, my naive self was quaking inside.

But then it came. 9:03 a.m., the reporter shouts, "OH MY GOD! A second plane has hit the second tower."

I felt as if I might vomit. My head was spinning. I suddenly imagined tanks roaming our streets as we hid in broken-down buildings and scavenged for food to survive. Isn't that what war-torn countries look like? My mom was born in the Great Depression and suffered from malnutrition. That was a stock market crash and not a war. Too many thoughts flooded my head and all of them were terrifying. Shaking myself out of the spiral, I knew I had to do two things. Get my children out of school and go home. I needed to be with my family. I needed to find peace in my God and His ability to protect us in this country from being a war-torn country.

I whispered to the nurse that I would like to call my kids. She looked at me with understanding. I knew by her look that she, too, would like to leave this room and make a phone call. But her task was here until this surgery and recovery were done. While on the phone with my husband and hearing that the children were already on their way home, the message came over the loudspeaker in the hospital that all non-essential people needed to exit the hospital. Relieved that I was non-essential, I quickly packed my things and walked away from the patient and his surgery with no thought other than what it would be like to wake up and find that your world has changed forever. I expected how the patient would feel was similar to how I felt. I felt like I was trying to wake myself from this nightmare. I felt so afraid of the images in my mind. *Could this really be happening in this country?*

Chapter Twenty-One
THE DAY MY HEART STOOD STILL

If you're going through hell, keep going.
—Winston Churchill

Walking to my car from the hospital, my heart raced almost as fast as my thoughts. Even the mild breeze and sunny skies of my home state of Florida could not pull me from the darkness of our world. Trying to reconcile my naivety with reality, I realized I was among those poor souls who were afraid. I got into my car and turned on the radio. Shaking and praying, I drove a few minutes down the road. At 9:37 a.m., more tragedy struck. I heard the Pentagon was hit as well. I cried out, "Dear God! How much more? Please stop this madness. Lord, please protect my family and loved ones."

As I drove home, I wept with agony over the things that were about to change that I didn't even understand yet. But I knew the innocence of my children was taken. TERRORISTS forever stole the belief that we lived in a protected country. I wanted to go into my quiet, safe world and pull the covers over my head, but my personal world was already far from safe or quiet. The man waiting for me to arrive home was no longer one who helped us feel any sense of calm. It was hard for me to imagine that just four years ago, our marriage was happy, and I was more in love with him than I had ever been. But now, I am driving into the unknown, as I did every day, but rather than just my war in my home, the world around me was turning upside down.

During the thirty minute drive home, I thought about what I might be driving into. I couldn't help but do some quick comparisons. Terrorists stirred fear in the heart of every American. James stirred fear in the heart of my children. My heart was breaking, and I was undone. How was this terrorist attack affecting them? I felt too much emotion, and I cried out to God. I needed wisdom from above to help them navigate this nightmare. I needed a moment's peace to be centered again and to ask God to intervene, to bring clarity and peace on how I would move forward from here. I silently prayed, *Be with me, Lord, give me Your words.*

As I walked into my home, the one that I hardly tolerated, I took a deep breath and prayed once more for peace. My house was clean but in an embarrassing state of disrepair. The driveway was a space of torn-up gravel with grass growing through and it stopped at what was once a carport but was now a family room. This was my home—the one that had more things wrong than were right. A three-bedroom, one-bath home that was 1100 square feet. I complained about the leaks, the broken window now taped with duct tape, and the ancient carpet, to name a few things. But, at this moment, the disrepair did not matter. Funny, the things that consume us can become so unimportant instantly. I just wanted to check on my children and see that everyone was home and as safe as anyone could be on 9/11.

Still dressed in white scrubs, I immediately surveyed the family room to account for each child. I noticed an extra child I did not know occupied the couches and stared wide-eyed at the TV—the clamor of voices announcing every known detail. President Bush had confirmed it was an apparent terrorist attack. Reports reminded us of the violence in 1993 when a bomb exploded in the World Trade Center parking garage. They knew in 1996 of the ties between Osama bin Laden and Al-Qaeda. People were suggesting that America was asleep when it shouldn't have been. Many predicted there would be another attack on the Twin Towers.

Fingers were already being pointed.

On their phones, bystanders got the first plane crashing into the tower on videos, which were airing on TV news programs. "Terrorist attack" kept playing in my head. How can it be? I live in THE United States of America. We have the greatest military in the world. My father often told me that he fought in Vietnam and Korea for our freedom so we could live without fear. Terrorist ATTACK? NOOOO! My mind wanted to reject the thought, but the reality was settling in my broken heart. An accident could not be two planes, let alone four.

Somberly, I walked to my small, overcrowded bedroom with a king-size bed, dresser, chest of drawers, and two nightstands to change my clothes. I had rich green on the walls in my bedroom and the hall was painted a celery green with white trim on the six doors in our short six-foot hallway. The peaceful, warm green made the hall to the bedrooms comforting. But this journey down the hall felt different. My heart was so heavy with questions I could not hear the Lord answering. My daughter Jenna followed close behind because she wanted to talk with me privately. She shut the door and locked it since a non-family member was in the home. I looked at her, and I could see the questions.

As I was still trying to think about how to open the conversation with her, my husband came down the hallway and found the door was locked. He started banging on the door with his fist and screaming, "You can't keep me out of MY room." Poisoned by my continued irritation with this man that he thought only of himself, mixed with the embarrassment I felt personally for myself and my children that this non-family member was witnessing the lunacy of their friend's father, my heart was racing and my pulse pounding. The terror of this day had overwhelmed my senses, and I was angry with his outburst on a level I could not put into words.

A scripture went through my mind: "A gentle answer deflects anger, but harsh words make tempers flare" (Proverbs 15:1 NLT). Even though I said nothing, the way I snatched the door open and glared at that madman…well, suffice it to say, it was not a soft answer.

I venomously said through gritted teeth, barely above a whisper, "Not today, James. I have one nerve left, and you are on it." But he came into the room saying repeatedly, at top volume, that I can't mistreat him because I think I am better than him. His face was so angry, and normally I would do anything to keep the children from being exposed to his barrage of verbal junk. But today, the cares of the world were so great that it just annoyed me that he had the audacity to believe that his little problem amounted to any of my concerns.

I had heard his accusations so many times in the early years of my married life. When James didn't get his way, he played pity party games. Although he never said this line from a thirteenth-century rhyme, "Nobody likes me, everybody hates me, I think I'll go eat worms," he acted in such a way that it proved he felt that way. When he got saved, this kind of manipulation abated. However, when he became disabled, it was fresh and new every morning.

Feeling that discreteness was not within me today, I sent Jenna from the room. She left looking dejected. Once more, her father was all-consuming, and nobody could spend time with me alone. Through gritted teeth, I said: "What is your problem? Do you not know that the world is going to hell in a handbasket right now, and you are making a big deal about a locked door that your daughter locked for privacy from another child?"

He started again with the whole, "you can't lock me out of my room" mantra.

I took a breath and more calmly repeated, "Jenna locked the door because I was undressing, and a child in the house was not ours." Thinking that if I worded it differently with a more tranquil tone, he could get it in his thick head and hear through the compulsive anger. I was wrong! He would not relent. He repeated his mantra, adding, "I should just go blow my brains out because nobody cares anything about me."

This six-foot man, who weighed nearly 290 pounds, was acting like a spoiled rotten brat. I felt overwhelmed by this adult child. I had a moment of insanity, or was it completely sane? I said, "Please do! Take the car and go to the lake. When you blow your brains out, you do it so that your children don't have to suffer any more of your nonsense." He was stunned. Admittedly, I, too, was stunned. I could see for the first time that my love had died. It was dead, and he had killed it. I was apathetic to his manipulative threats, but this wasn't a new threat! It was one I had heard many times over the years. He would thrust his guilt on my heart to settle me down. Though it had worked in all the other past times to get me to give up on my position—not today!

Today was a day with other things to deal with. Today I had to think about my children and how to make them feel safe. The world we knew was spinning out of control, and I could not conjure up a single shred of care for his pathetic pity party.

After briefly pausing in his tirade to think about what just happened and to search his thoughts to say something new to move me from this contemptuous position, he said, "Maybe I just need to be locked up." Wasn't it interesting that he no longer spoke of killing himself? Why did he change when I encouraged him to do it?

I no longer begged or cared. "Just do it already. I don't want to deal with this anymore." Then a new thought stirred. I thought, *Why did I not see this before? He never intended to kill himself. He has always been about controlling me.* After all the years of being manipulated by that threat, finally, I understood, and maybe for the first time in my life, he never had any plans to harm himself. That's why he switched his threat so quickly to being locked up.

He repeated this new threat, "Maybe I just need to be locked up."

My mind filled with the prospect of having James out of the picture for a few days and how wonderful it would be to have time with my kids without his constant need to be the center of attention. I needed to be able to talk with my teenagers without fear that they would say something that he would hear, making him angry enough to verbally attack their already fragile emotions. Truly it sounded like a dream. Formulating a plan, I said, "Yes, I think you do."

Don't get me wrong. James was no more suicidal than I was, but I knew if I got my pastor to take him, he would be held for seventy-two glorious hours. We all needed that break. I went to the phone in the bedroom and called my pastor. He knew well the issues of our home. I told him about the conversation, and he asked if I wanted him to come and pick James up and take him to the psych hospital. "Why yes, yes, I do," I said, with a small hint of guilt. I knew James' modus operandi was manipulation and not self-harm. However, they didn't know that yet!

I told James to pack whatever he wanted to take for three days. I knew there was no danger of him being admitted over those three days because he was not and never will be suicidal. He was just selfish and self-centered and felt sorry for himself. I told him his wish was coming true today. He would be the center of attention. He would be their highest priority.

Honestly, I did not take the time to pray and ask God about my decision; I was just desperate to get back to what I needed most—time with my teenagers. I just wanted some peace, and I was angry. So angry! And SO tired! Full-time nursing school, three part-time jobs, three teenagers, and a crazy needy husband was taking its toll on my forty-one-year-old self.

About forty minutes later, our pastor picked James up. Oddly, James didn't seem upset. I wondered if he wasn't just a little happy to get the attention that he so desperately craved.

The first night without James was excellent. With the quiet home and the extra child returning to her house, I took the kids to Wendy's and discussed the day's events. It was weird at Wendy's. The commonly packed fast-food restaurant was quiet and empty. There was a normal number of employees but no other customers. We had the dining room to ourselves.

There was an eerie quiet as the radio played in the kitchen, with news feeds repeating every detail and discussing every opinion as to why this had happened. Everyone was glued to new reports. As we took our seats in the dining room, we talked about where we were when we found out what had happened. Who had told each person, and how? And more importantly, how did they feel when they heard the news? The kids described the principal coming on the intercom, saying something vague like there was an attack in New York, and out of an abundance of caution, they were sending all kids home. We discussed how we were feeling about the uncertainties.

The kids felt confused. That was a common feeling among most people in those early moments following this horrific tragedy. They questioned their safety and wondered why they needed to come home from school. What a good question. I talked about how the Bible says to trust God because He alone is our Protector. We don't have to trust the military or government, but we can trust God.

The conversation with my kids went on for more than an hour. Then I prayed, feeling so heavy yet knowing the truth about the need to trust God and His protection—just as I told them. I talked about how no matter what is happening or what we think or feel, God is with us and will never leave or forsake us. I distinctly remember praying that fear would not grip us, even though I was struggling to keep any faith working within me. But I felt an odd peace after that prayer. I knew we would be okay. It seemed a preposterous thought, but somehow, the Living God assured me that we would fear no evil even if I felt black clouds looming around me and walking in the shadow of death, FOR HE IS WITH US! I BELIEVE!! It doesn't matter what I feel or don't feel. It doesn't matter what I think or don't think. It doesn't matter what I see or don't see. His Word says He will not abandon me, and I will trust Him.

Chapter Twenty-Two
GUILT-RIDDEN

There is no greater sorrow
than to recall happiness in times of misery.
—Dante Alighieri

Sleep was peaceful that night. I knew my loving Abba Father was with us and would be with us through whatever happened. I just needed to keep putting one foot in front of the other. When I woke, I wondered how the world would be different today. Schools were open, although that was under great debate. Everyone tried to decide if they felt safe enough to allow their children to go. Being in Florida seemed safe enough to me, and besides, since I was in nursing school and had no choice about going to class, I wanted them in school and not home alone.

I pulled into the college parking lot for my typical Wednesday class; it was as if the world was the same as it was the day before at this same time. Resuming my normal life when the world was in chaos felt surreal. A news channel was playing on nearly every TV on campus. Yesterday by 10 a.m., there was not a person alive that didn't know about the terrorist attack. It was as if the world stood still, and all eyes were glued to their television or radio. Everyone was talking about the attacks.

Today on this college campus, the typical chatter could not be heard. The normal robust banter, wisecracks, and even complaining about tests were replaced with the feel of a funeral. It was like every person on the campus had lost a personal loved one in that attack—the urge to cry was not far from many as we all walked an emotional tightrope.

Because phone lines and cell towers were jammed with calls to New York, many people had not heard from loved ones to know if they were alright, and the unknown was heavy in the air. Tears of fear mixed with tears of loss for those who already knew reminded us of how terrifying the world could be. And with the loss this significant, it would take a long while to heal. Overhearing one conversation as I passed, a lady was waiting and hoping to get word about her sister who worked in the towers, but she still hadn't heard. I admit, my heart broke for the most likely reason.

As terrible as the news was on every front, I woke with joy. *How could I feel joy in a time like this? How dare I feel happy when the world is in chaos?* I had awoken to no argument, no demand for my attention, no yelling about being overlooked. Wow. We got up this morning in peace. I got my coffee, packed my bag, got the kids out the door, and left for school without a fight. I couldn't remember a less eventful, wonderful time. I might have even heard the birds singing if I hadn't felt so guilty about being so happy James was not there. But I did feel guilty. Even with the joy I felt, the guilt stole my ability to relax and breathe. I was a mess. I tried to console myself that I was walking in a place of trust that God would protect us, and I didn't need to feel guilty about that. But I knew the truth. Hardly a day had passed in over a year that my morning was peaceful. *Why did I feel so guilty for being happy?*

The news grew heavier as the day moved forward on the ghostly empty college campus. I had no personal connection to anyone in New York. However, many Floridians are related to New Yorkers. I felt their loss. I began, though, to see we were not so different. My husband was not in the twin towers in New York, but he was missing. The shell that looked like my loving husband and the wonderful father to our three children was no longer present. He, too, had succumbed to the crumbling of a structure.

I walked into class and took my seat. As usual, I was first to arrive. Today was a test day, and I was ready, but I always sat quietly and perused the material just before the test for any last-minute nuggets I could glean. But not today. I just stared out the window at the people walking to their classes. Gone were the typical gaieties. The halls seemed more like a library—with quiet conversations in the corners, and one person who was crying.

My attention returned to the classroom as my classmate and friend arrived. She commented how weird it felt to come on campus today with such quietness. We discussed the events of the previous day. She told me about her OR clinical experience. The group she was with were readying a woman for surgery when word spread. They, too, were sent home as "non-essential." She said the woman heard the announcement and learned of the terrorist attacks. I wondered what it might have felt like to be a patient getting ready for anesthesia, and not knowing what you would wake up to in your world. The thought was terrifying. At least my patient went to sleep without thinking of a world crisis.

The situation we faced just after 9/11 reminded me of the scripture that says, "While people are saying, 'Peace and safety,' destruction will come on them suddenly, as labor pains on a pregnant woman, and they will not escape" (1 Thessalonian 5:3 NIV). Even though this scripture is referring to the End Times when Jesus comes back, we were most definitely living the truth of this scripture on 9/11. Never, before 9/11, do I remember feeling such uncertainty.

Shaken from my thoughts, the professor was calling for our attention. She had the dubious task of sympathizing with where our hearts and thoughts might be, but she had a schedule to keep. Life must move on! The test was given out, and we all focused on the task of completing it. After this test and two lectures, it was time to go home. Only then did my thoughts return to James. I wondered what was happening in the psych hospital. *Could they possibly see him as a threat to himself and keep him?* I was sure I knew the answer to my question, but that didn't stop the silent prayer that they would. I called and spoke with a nurse who updated me on his path, but there was much to do before making any determinations.

Feeling like time was running out in my reprieve from him, I went to the store and paid money I didn't have to spend to buy food to make a special dish for the kids. I rented a movie I knew they would like. Over dinner, we discussed our day and various experiences in our respective environments. We discussed what the media was reporting and the dreaded pictures that everyone was talking about.

Desperate to use the time to have fun, I made a stupid joke, and we did enjoy humor we hadn't been able to experience in quite some time. After clowning around, we cleared the table and watched the movie. I felt happy down to my core. It felt odd to have so much happiness and joy when the world was in chaos. However, there was joy and peace, living in the moment, at home with my children in a stress-free environment, and the cares of the world seemed far away.

The next day I awakened with gratitude for an evening of contentment. With a quick prayer, I was off to school early for a study date with my friend, Amy. She was the sweetest, smartest girl, with her own beautiful little girl at home that was as adorable as her mom.

Amy didn't talk much about home. I knew she lived with her father, but I suspected a boyfriend was somewhere in the picture because sometimes she would wear heavy makeup to hide the bruises, which were never really hidden. I asked her about it once, and she quickly brushed aside the question and only commented that she just needed to get through nursing school, and then everything would be all right. She made it clear that she would not talk about it. I often prayed for her and tried to be the best friend she could have. I told her I would always be a safe place for her to talk openly. She still chose silence.

The atmosphere had improved on campus. After only forty-eight hours, it seemed people had found a way to push past the grief and accomplish the daily grind. Though the news continued to be filled with so much devastation, the coverage of people pulled from the rubble began taking center stage. In particular, there was much focus on two Port Authority Police officers, McLoughlin and Jimeno, who were buried beneath thirty feet of rubble for twenty-four hours but were rescued.

In total, twenty survivors were pulled from the rubble, the last being twenty-seven hours after the attack. The celebration of the lives saved was barely heard before recorded conversations of others trapped in the wreckage making their last phone calls to their loved ones before they succumbed to their last breath—too many tears in those first days. Again, guilt came up in my throat as my tiny world felt so wonderful. But, as if to say, "Not so fast, Donna," I got a phone call from the psych hospital.

Chapter Twenty-Three

ALL THINGS ARE POSSIBLE WITH GOD

*"The Lord God is your leader,
and he will fight for you with his mighty miracles"
Deuteronomy 1:30 TLB*

The social worker had some disastrous news for me. James confessed to some of his bad behaviors, which resulted in a Department of Human Services (DHS) investigation of the safety of my children in my home. The peace was gone, and the rage was back, clouding my ability to think clearly. James often performed the Goliath act to scare us into submission. However, not one time did he ever hit or injure any of us—physically that is!

When he was asked why I was angry with him, he told the counselor, "For things like when I threw the coffee table across the room at our son out of anger."

He had to tell them that? He couldn't tell them about the millions of times he had threatened to kill himself because we didn't act the way he wanted. He couldn't tell them he was constantly negative and a drain on the happiest moments. He had to bring up throwing a coffee table. He did throw the coffee table in the direction of Jarred, but he never intended to hit Jarred with the coffee table. It was more of a, "look how mighty I am, don't cross me" type of display. It was the kind James favored. James was into mental abuse, not physical abuse. Unfortunately, the emotional bloody nose and bruises are just as painful, perhaps more so, because they cannot be seen on the body and therefore do not elicit compassion or understanding from others. James was careful and, dare I say, proud to say that he never hit us as if to imply that it made his behavior less painful.

I panicked when the counselor told me James was being released from the facility. According to personnel at the facility, he was not supposed to be around the children until the investigation was over. I had no place to send him. The facility didn't provide anywhere for him to go. I had already tried to send him to his mother's one time so we could get a break. He was there less than two weeks when she had had enough and sent him back. James' brother said she nearly had a breakdown in those nine days. I was stuck with him, and despite the facility's request, there was no way to keep him from the children. To keep us all safe and sane, we used the only powerful weapon we had: prayer.

I was terrified about what that would mean. I prayed without ceasing. I called Nelson, but he didn't have any real ideas either. I was trapped, so he prayed that God would intervene somehow.

The next afternoon, Pastor Jason picked up James and brought him home. He talked with him about what he was doing to his family. James repented. When I got home, we discussed the concerns that he was not supposed to be in our home. He thought it was ridiculous because he said, "I have never laid a hand on anyone." There it was! His badge of honor making all his actions okay. His idea of abuse was only physical. Not that it was a shocker, but we needed a plan. We decided that when the social worker called, he would leave on his scooter and travel the neighborhood until the social worker left. Anyone who knows how social workers work knows they don't announce when they are coming, a fact that I did not know at the time.

So, one sunny afternoon I was studying at the dining room table, and a knock came at the door. I opened it to a charming woman with kind eyes who introduced herself as the social worker investigating the claim. Between the panic, the praying, and the terror shredding my insides, she calmly asked where she could meet with each child independently.

James was sitting in the family room watching TV. He was not in clear view, and I didn't mention he was there. I sent her to my bedroom, where I knew she might spot James when she came from the bedroom, but I prayed she would not. One by one, she took the children into my room. I sat on the porch praying and half threatening God. If you don't have her rule in my favor God, and she takes my children away, I am going to prison for murder tonight. That man will not take one more thing from me. I could sense God trying to get through my thoughts with some reason for my soul, but I could not calm myself and listen.

Nearly an hour had passed, and my body was weak with the adrenaline coursing through my veins as the social worker emerged from the house to where I was on the porch. I stood, and she put her arm on my shoulders and started walking me away from our home. She whispered, "You certainly have a mess here and a complicated life." With my eyes wide but almost afraid to look at her, she continued, "I don't know what you're doing, but each of your children is very confident that you would not let anything happen to them. I am leaving here today, and you will not see me back. The case is closed."

Immediately, a water faucet unleashed in a slow trickle from my eyes. She smiled, hugged me, got in her car, and left. Then tears came full flow to wash away the adrenaline hammering at my heart. I was filled with glorious gratitude. God had come into this home and performed an impossible miracle. I shall never know if she knew James was in the house or God had just hidden him. But either way, I was so grateful for the outcome.

Suddenly, I saw the value in some of the hard steps Nelson had me take to provide security for my children: Requiring me to carry a cell phone so the children could always reach me, the weekly family meeting in my bedroom without James, and the extra adults to pour into each of their lives individually, all helped them feel secure. I felt the need to repent for not readily remembering the blessings in front of me. I praised the Lord for the wisdom of obeying those hard recommendations that made them feel safe. I knew, here and now, was the reason He led me to do those things. He went before me and behind me. He prepares a table before me in the presence of my enemies. While I could not see what tomorrow holds, I know who holds tomorrow! The God of Possible.

Chapter Twenty-Four

DESPAIR AND HOPELESS REVISIT

You can believe for the best in someone,
but nothing will change until they believe!
—Donna Bess

I am not sure why I was surprised, but the old James was back as soon as the crisis was over. No longer did he try to be nice. I just could not understand why he could make the choice to be kind when it was required by DHS but no longer when they were not a threat. The children were here to stay, and now he was free to act the way he felt most like himself. Our world was still in the throes of 9/11. It had only been three weeks, and I already felt like I had died, was raised from the dead, and killed again. I was struggling with my inability to stay positive in our soul-crushing life. The roller coaster of emotions and life's demands was taking its toll.

Oh, don't get me wrong. Nursing school was going well. In that environment, I was just Donna, the student. At home, I was Donna, who lives with a tormentor, and my capacity to love James anyway seemed to have died with those in the towers on 9/11. Before that point, I prayed for God to move James' heart to love his children. And me, too, for that matter. I prayed for miracles and for healing of his heart issues that were stealing life from him. But honestly, I didn't even care about me anymore. I so desperately wanted to protect the father/child relationship from being permanently fractured in the eyes of my precious children.

But on that day, the day the world stood still—the day that the eyes of every person in every nation were glued to their televisions, I was awakened to a revelation. A demonically developed plan to destroy innocent lives was being lived out on our televisions and in our country on the worst day in our lifetime, and even that could not get James' eyes off himself. I wondered, *What is the point of my prayers?*

Something shifted in me that day. Hopelessness for change had moved into my heart. There would be no more crying out for restoring relationships with his children. No more hopeful words of encouragement. I was angry and hurt, and I was done. His quick change before the investigation and immediate reversal sealed the deal. It wrecked me. What I saw with my eyes ruined my ability to believe that James would change. He didn't want to. God doesn't make someone change who is unwilling. He gave Adam and Eve a choice in the garden. We get a choice about how we behave as well. James had made his choice.

This revelation necessitated that I shift my focus from trying to create right relationships in our home to walking in God's divine protection and receiving healing from the traumas suffered, as much as that depended on me. I no longer cajoled and pleaded with James to be kind. It was time to pull up our armor and ride this out. He would either change or God would take him. I encouraged the children to do the same. "See your father's poison as fiery darts that God extinguishes when they hit God's shield. God can protect you even when your father blasts."

You and I both know that is ridiculous. With their dying breath, children will always look to their parents for approval. Nothing can change that. They want it and need it. Even as adults, if we are honest, we want and need approval from our parents. A grievous fracture of the relationship can squash the need. But the desire is forever alive. Our natural desire is to have that, even if it will never be. But at the time just after 9/11, I had no other words. I was empty. I just needed to focus on things I could affect—my children and nursing school.

You may want to judge my calloused heart, or maybe you are right there with me in your struggle. But what I have to share next is so important, so please stay with me and listen to the rest of his cancer journey.

At this point in my story, I truly felt like I hated James. His insecurity had grown to epic proportions. It would be impossible to tell you everything that happened because there would be volumes and volumes of unkind stories about a man I deeply loved. So rather, I would like to tell you why those unkind stories happened.

Chapter Twenty-Five
PRODUCTS OF DYSFUNCTION

Dysfunction will result when your identity is formed on a corrupt foundation of untruths.
—Donna Bess

According to The Institute of Counseling, "A dysfunctional family is one whose interrelationships serve to detract from, rather than promote, the emotional and physical health and well-being of its members."[4] James grew up in a dysfunctional home where they tried to love; however, dysfunctional people often have not had love demonstrated, so becoming a loving person is a large challenge. James' home as a child was filled with anger, guns, alcohol, and pornography. His mother was kind, but his father was an alcoholic, easily driven to rage. She was timid about engaging with James' father, and she just tried to keep the peace—a condition I understood all too well.

When James and I got engaged, his parents tried to talk him out of marrying me. My father ran his own construction company, and they were doing okay financially. His parents told James that I was born with a silver spoon in my mouth, and they didn't like my kind because it would change him.

First, I was not born with a silver spoon in my mouth; my military father worked very hard and served in war three times while we struggled for our daily existence. I remember one Christmas when we had a barren tree with only a single gift under the tree. It was a much-needed sweater for me. They promised to give my two older brothers a little cash the next pay period. We often ate dented sea rations for dinner because we had no money. Most military families were just like us and not a silver spoon among us.

When my dad retired from the military, he bounced to a few types of jobs before he settled in construction. By the time I was in high school, he had his own construction company and was financially stable. I had nice clothes, and I drove a new car. However, I paid for all that with money from my full-time job. Still, no silver spoon, just hard work.

James and I married against their wishes. The first two years of our marriage were laced with hardships imposed by his family. Many middle-of-the-night phone calls would wake us. His drunken father or upset brother would call James to look for his mom. They fought, and she left on foot in the country's dark night. They needed James to look for her and bring her home. This was because James' father was drunk and could not drive. James would get up, drive thirty-five miles to where they lived, and start driving all the streets to find his mom on the dark road in the very rural area. He took her home, and then he would try to talk things down for the next hour. Then he would drive thirty-five miles back home and have an hour or so before he had to get up and go to work.

One night, I reached my limit. I told James that he should move back home with them if he allowed them to take another night of our sleep to manage their marital problems. It was ridiculous that these grown people called their nineteen-year-old son to take care of their problems. Mature people don't pull their kids into their matrimonial issues for a resolution.

He considered what I said and called them back. He told them they would need to resolve their issues on their own. He had to work, and he needed some sleep. I was happy, even though James' boundary fostered a greater flow of hate from his parents toward me.

At one point, James' father got so angry at me that he picked up a rifle, cocked it, and pointed straight at me and my swollen belly, carrying his first grandchild. James jumped off the couch and stood between his dad and me. He talked his dad down from the ledge. I always felt they hated me and now that thought was confirmed. So, when I say hate, I mean hate in every sense of the word. Suffice it to say; they did everything they could to tear me down in James' eyes.

His father told me never to come back to their home. I wish I could tell you that demand made me sad. But who wants to be anywhere they know in no uncertain terms that they are despised? I didn't ever want to go back to their house. However, the problem arose because James continued to go weekend after weekend. He said that just because I couldn't be there didn't mean he should stay away. I felt he chose them over me since all his off time was with them, rather than his pregnant wife. To me, that was the essence of dysfunction. What else can it be called when a husband chooses to spend his off time with a family that refuses to have his wife around?

Things changed a bit when Mindy was born. James' parents wanted to see their grandchild. I would not allow my baby in their home without me. They conceded and "allowed me to come so they could see their grandchild." This ridiculously unhealthy relationship continued until I received the greatest gift of my life—Jesus. Although the hate they showed me did not change, something did. I never again felt threatened by his dad. I believed it was the protection of the Holy Spirit. When his dad was about to lose it on me, he would walk out to the barn and do target practice with his multiple guns. I can only imagine whose face was on those targets.

I began to see the real issues for James and his dad. First, they did not know Christ. Aside from not knowing the gentle Father and Savior, we all have probably suffered from low self-esteem on some level. And for many of us, we still do, even after we know His love. For James and his dad, low self-esteem was manifested by a lot of blame-shifting to remain in control. The need to feel in control was behind many of their statements and actions.

Because James and his parents saw apologies as a sign of weakness, they did not feel the need to apologize for anything. Also, if, for some reason, anyone did do or say anything that seemed to upset their sense of control, they made sure to point out that person's shortcomings or mistakes to put them back in their place.

This kind of thinking is poison in every relationship, and these kinds of thoughts will never bring health and wholeness. Nor will they lead us to be what God calls us to be. And, perhaps most importantly, they nearly guarantee to produce unhealthy fruit. When we mistreat others, we reap mistreatment in return. If I was going to stop this harmful exchange, I had to stop getting sidetracked by my hurt feelings, which continued the same broken cycle.

God says that I have the mind of Christ (1 Corinthians 2:16). That means I have the intelligence, gifts, and talents that God has given me, and to deny that I have these things, is to deny God.

I learned to surrender my emotions to the "mind of Christ" to respond, rather than react, to the purposefully hurtful things that were said to me. The people who said hurtful things didn't have the mind of Christ. I could not expect that of them. My only choice was to learn to allow the Spirit of God to protect my heart and to let all my words be gentle. I'm not joking when I tell you this was a struggle. But I took comfort from the fact that, "The LORD will accomplish what concerns me" (Psalm 138:8 NASB). Notice there is no "I" in that statement. I could not walk in those truths. But the Spirit of God could do that in me. Over time, I got better at letting God fight my battles.

As you may recall, neither James nor I knew Christ when we married. The foundation of our identity was in what we did and how we looked to others. I didn't understand that marrying someone who had a wrecked sense of identity meant they would transfer that shakable foundation to you and expect you to make it stable. Relationships are hard work for healthy individuals. But add the responsibility of making your spouse feel good about who he or she is—that is impossible! This dynamic is especially difficult when one spouse is responsible for helping the other feel good about himself all while the other person is tearing the responsible one down to fill the very need the other person is trying so hard to meet. Because I too was struggling with my own sense of value, I failed miserably at helping James with his identity in those early years.

As for my husband's parents, low self-esteem continued to steal from them throughout their lives. Shortly before my father-in-law died of lung cancer, he summoned me to his home. I sat across the kitchen table, and he reached for my hands. I gave them freely. I have tears even now. This man never showed a single thought or act of compassion toward me in the fourteen years he had been in my life. But here in the kitchen, I knew something was different.

With tears, he said, "We haven't always agreed." We both got a small chuckle from the understatement. He continued, "But you are good for Jimmy, and I know you are the best thing that ever happened to him."

At that moment, I was reminded of a statement James' Aunt Lynette spoke to me just a couple of years into our marriage. She said, "I know the family does not like you, but you are good for this family. Just keep being you." She hugged me as she drove out of our driveway. She died of a heart attack a year or so later.

Sitting across the table from my father-in-law, listening to discover why I was summoned, I realized this was a plea for forgiveness even if the words never came. My heart was open as he continued to speak, "I find myself worried about the other two children and their families, but you and Jimmy will be all right. Your faith is strong."

I had no words…just tears. I hugged him and answered back with a choked-up voice, "Thank you!" He died weeks later.

But that day, as I drove home, tears welled from gratitude. Somehow, I felt redeemed and not hated. A heaviness was lifted, and all the years of trying to measure every word or phrase in their presence seemed to have a happy ending. We did find out at the funeral; the hospice chaplain had led him to the Lord a few months before he died. Great relief washed over us.

Knowing his father came to the Lord helped turn James into the husband that was my life partner, my lover, my friend, and confidant. Before James' father passed, James knowing the Lord had brought only minor changes. But the change he saw in his dad had a greater impact. James started walking in greater truth and love. Our marriage turned into something beautiful. We were the happiest we had been in years. We had rejoiced in the Lord and each other.

However, cancer took whatever strength James had to make different choices. Despite my prayers and pleas, James did not surrender his self-focus. I knew he was hurting, yet the only answer I had for him, he seemed to reject. I felt powerless to change the course. I longed to have my husband back. I wished and prayed for the kind and loving father for my children to resurface. If only my love, still hidden deep in my wounded heart, could make a difference.

Chapter Twenty-Six

LOSING MYSELF TO CHANGE

Storms change the terrain of your soul.
If the foundation isn't solid, destruction results.
—Donna Bess

I was entering the home stretch for nursing school. James had not changed his unhappy disposition. His anger was among the top challenges in life for our family. My mom invited me to come for a visit to her home in North Carolina during spring break. I was desperate for a break, and I managed to get James' mom to stay with James. Mindy and Jarred had to work. That meant one glorious week of escape. Jenna, my youngest daughter, and I drove excitedly to spend a week with Granny, who would spoil Jenna immensely while I selfishly laid around reading for pleasure. I had historical fiction novels beckoning me to visit places I only knew in my dreams. I had collected novels in the last year, when I was fully engaged in classes and textbooks, to be enjoyed "someday." My "someday" collection was packed, and we were ready.

Our first full day at my mom's was perfect. I slept and read one entire novel and part of another with cat naps here and there while Mom and Jenna spent the day out shopping, eating lunch, and visiting some places Mom loved to go. It was quiet, peaceful, and a tremendous blessing. I only came out of my room when Mom and

Jenna came home for the evening, and we enjoyed a wonderful dinner together with lots of laughter. The next few days, I did venture out a bit more for some of Mom's planned excursions with Jenna, but mostly, I stayed in my room reading. Something about visiting other lands and escaping my life by living vicariously through other people's lives in those books brought me pleasure, and the frequent cat naps brought rest to my weary soul. Since I only averaged four to six hours of sleep every night for a year, I reveled in the slumber.

We went out to lunch on the last day before I needed to return to reality. I felt refreshed and ready to return to my home, school, and work life. At lunch, we laughed much about nothing. My soul was full. I explained what a gift it had been for Jenna and me to be with her. "Mom, I am so grateful for you." I told her that her constant care for me had helped sustain me in the darkest times. She teared up. With graduation only one-and-a-half semesters away, we discussed vacations together. Maybe even a Christmas cruise. Mom and I love cruises. It would be hard to say goodbye in the morning, but the time had been filled with many moments of joy.

After lunch, I needed to go to the bank to get cash to travel home the next day. I was driving Mom's car, she was in the passenger seat, and Jenna was in the back seat behind Mom when I saw a blue streak out of nowhere, and our car slammed to a sudden stop, seemingly in the middle of the road. With a hard lurch forward in our seats and an equally hard slam back, the car settled. I had no idea how it happened, but we had just been in a car crash.

As the car filled with smoke, I was afraid there was a fire. Jenna screamed in the back seat, "I can't move my legs!" Jenna already had a cast from her knee down on one leg from a broken bone, so I wondered if something had happened to that injury. I jumped from the car and ran to Mom and Jenna's side.

First, checking on Jenna, who was utterly hysterical, repeating, "I can't feel my legs."

After a quick assessment, I believed she was okay, but the seatbelt was jammed. I told her to sit still; the paramedics would be here shortly. I then went to Mom's side, who was moaning. In my panic, I gently shook her, "Mom, are you okay?"

Mom's first and only words came through shortness of breath that left me numb. "I'm not going to make it out of this one, Donna."

I cried out, "Mom, please don't say that." Tears spilling quietly from my eyes, trying to stay strong, I began to pray with a fervency that was part passion and trust and part a panicked plea for her to survive. She was the one in my family of origin left in my life that loved me. Our relationship was the best it had ever been. She was my friend and surely God would not take her. I needed her.

Before I knew it, many police and EMS people were surrounding us. We were in a zone where the school was about to let out. The axle from Mom's car was blocking the driveway into the school. It was a frenzied scene everywhere I looked, but none of the madness could compete with the chaos of my little world. I was terrified. Jenna panicked; Mom was still moaning and had spoken no more words. Being hustled away from the car so the emergency personnel could converge on the passengers, I felt weak in my knees. Perhaps a bit of déjà vu, most likely adrenaline, driving the desire to pass out. But deep breaths helped to keep me focused on what was happening around me.

Standing where I could see Mom and Jenna, I watched as they loaded Mom into the ambulance. She was no longer responsive. Jenna was now a bit calmer since they explained to her that her legs were fine. She was just in shock from the seatbelt. I stood next to Jenna as they cut the seatbelt and got her onto a backboard. They told her it was a precaution, and they were taking her to the hospital. I certainly hoped so. I felt the same way, but at this point, I wasn't sure what was knowledge and what was wishful thinking. After Jenna was loaded into the ambulance, the focus turned toward me. "I'm fine," I said to the paramedic.

He looked at the car on the driver's side that was missing the whole front of the vehicle right up to my door and said, "How about you let me be the judge of that." It took some firm convincing, but he convinced me to let him look at me. Only then did I realize my left arm was hanging and turning multiple shades of purple. When he asked about my arm, and I looked at it, I almost felt like it had to belong to someone else. It indeed looked like it would be painful, but I felt nothing. They insisted on taking me to the hospital as well.

As the paramedic got me on the stretcher to put in the ambulance, I heard what had happened. At about 2 p.m., a drunk driver lost control of his car and hit four vehicles, sending one sailing into oncoming traffic in the opposite direction. The blue streak I saw was a blue minivan that bolted before me with no time to react. That explains how the axle became detached from our car. Once the vehicle stopped, the smoke I thought might be fire was the powder from the airbags filling the cabin. The three other vehicles involved had minor injuries requiring no trips to the hospital.

Once we arrived at the hospital, they checked me out and found I had severe tendonitis, and the bruising was because I was on a blood thinner. My chest and abdomen also became a massive bruise from neck to lap line where the seatbelt caught me. A very short time and an X-ray later, I was released with pain medications.

Jenna already had a broken leg when we left for the trip, and her leg numbness was from the seatbelt. The ER physician told her that if she had not been wearing a seatbelt in the backseat, at the rate of bruises, he could tell she would have taken her grandmother's head off on her way out the front windshield. Wow. That explains why I never had a problem getting her to keep her seatbelt on.

Mom was not so lucky. The airbags crushed her osteoporotic chest and punctured both lungs. The doctor told me every organ was bruised, and they needed to put her on a ventilator to allow the organs to heal. My brother, Don, who lived in the same town as my mom, and I stood looking at her, and the world felt hopeless. I cried with such anguish. I needed my mom. We had talked every day for the past eighteen months. She was the main person I counted on to help me emotionally. She listened, encouraged, and told me how proud she was of me, that I was strong, and that I amazed her. I needed her. She must live.

That night as Jenna and I were back at Mom's home, it was quiet. It felt overwhelming being in her home without her. Jenna sat with a distant look in her eyes and a constant flow of tears as she stared into the distance, no doubt trapped in the memory of the day's events. She wanted to go home. I could not imagine the pain of this sweet fifteen-year-old girl watching this horrible accident with her beloved "Granny" fighting for her life.

I prayed about it and talked with a few people. Many thought I should stay. Some said I should do what I felt was right, but intimated that I should stay. I was torn because I didn't want to leave Mom. I also didn't want to worry about the disabled husband at home. And probably a more significant point: I didn't want to get kicked out of school, which would happen if I didn't show up on Monday.

Late into the evening, Jenna was still in shock. I was...I don't know what I was, probably in shock. I couldn't believe this was happening. How was I supposed to make this decision? Each option left my heart torn. Leaving meant not being there with my mother, which was where I desperately wanted to be. But staying meant I needed to figure out what to do with James. His mom would not stay longer. I also knew the rules of nursing school. I would not be allowed to remain in the program. Our family needed a steady income, and I was so close to the end. How could this be happening? We were making plans today for a vacation. I wept!

As I was on the phone with James, I could not stop looking at Jenna's face. She had not said much in the hours since that dreadful scene, but in a quiet whimper, she had said a few times, "Mom, I just want to go home." At about 10 p.m., I decided to take her home the next day. It was not a popular decision with my family. Many family members made it known to me with no mincing of words, but I knew it was the right thing.

Because my brother lived in the same town as my mom, he would be able to manage things for her. I had a whole world of issues waiting for me at home, but more importantly, Jenna, my baby girl, had a world filled with tragedy between her father and now her grandmother. She needed what could not be filled in this empty house that was a constant reminder of what was missing. I needed to get my baby girl home to family and friends that provided a network of support.

Mom was in the Intensive Care Unit for nearly two months before it was time to send her to rehab to try to wean her off the ventilator. They were successful after weeks of false attempts, and we were finally starting to believe she could recover. I wanted desperately to speak with her, but she was not cognitively able to do that. I prayed without ceasing.

Meanwhile, I returned to school. One night, as if our Faithful Father heard my heart cry, James, myself, and our three children had a fantastic dinner. I don't remember what we ate, but I remember the atmosphere. The evening was perfect and one of complete joy. No anger, no yelling, no criticism, just great conversation and lots of laughter. At that time, we each received a gift of joy. I FELT EMOTIONALLY SATISFIED AND HAPPY when I got up to start cleaning—maybe even with a pep in my step. It was a miracle.

When dinner was over, and the kids retreated to their rooms to work on homework, I started cleaning the kitchen. As I was clearing the dishes, I was filled with such gratefulness. This meal had been a gift and some much-needed encouragement in the journey. Suddenly, there was a crash to the ground. I had heard James fall several times, and while it had to be James again, it was different. A groan followed the sound. We all went running in, and James was moaning on the floor. He had tripped over his shoe that he had left lying in his path.

I shook him, and he looked at me. He was aroused enough that Jarred and I were able to help him sit up and lean against the wall. James was unstable anyway, and it didn't take much to topple him. He had fallen before, so I was not overly concerned, but I watched because something seemed different. And then there was a change in his eyes. It seemed like he saw something in the distance instead of looking at us. I knew he was in trouble. I called 911.

By the time we reached the hospital, James was becoming unresponsive. The CAT Scan showed bleeding in his brain. That, combined with the brain tumor, was disastrous. The surgeon came around midnight and said they would watch him through the night and see if the bleeding would stop.

The next afternoon I had a nursing school clinical; fortunately, it was in the same hospital. I was able to check on James on my breaks. At about noon, the surgeon called me to meet him for a conversation. It was time to decide if I wanted to sign a DNR (Do Not Resuscitate) or take him for surgery. The results of surgery, of course, offered no guarantees. The surgeon felt surgery would only stop the bleeding, but it may not reverse what had already happened.

After many hours of praying, talking with my children, and even with my instructor, who had been brought into this scene, I signed the DNR. Late that evening, I sat in the waiting room with a sense of palpable brokenness and loss. This was it. I was giving up. I was laying down any remaining hope that James would make things right with his children. Sitting in that recliner in the waiting room, I laid down all my expectations—as well as everything I had clung to.

And then, as if that was not enough, my brother called from North Carolina with a report on my mom. She was not doing well, and we had to decide whether to put her back on a ventilator or sign a DNR. *God, what is happening right now? What are You doing?* Mom never mentally returned to us after she was off the ventilator; we decided it was time to give her peace.

Five days later, my sweet mom's body was flown to Florida to be buried next to my dad. My heart hurt. James was still in the hospital; as luck would have it, the bleeding stopped on its own, and he was doing much better. I debated telling him about Mom, and I decided against it.

On June 18, 2002, we were standing at the graveside of my precious Mom and saying our final goodbye. I needed her, and my heart was breaking without her. After the funeral, when everyone was leaving the graveside to head back to my house, I stood staring at the hole in the ground where her body would rest. Knowing she would be with Jesus when I got there was not bringing me much comfort. I needed her now. I needed to talk with her. Pastor Jason stood with me.

After a moment, he asked if I was going back home now or to the hospital to see James. Pulling myself out of the empty hole in the ground that felt like my soul, I responded, "James and I need to have a difficult conversation." I knew it would be a complicated conversation, and I was not looking forward to it. I needed to tell him I could no longer care for him at home. His needs were becoming too great. Pastor Jason asked if I wanted him to come, and I quickly jumped at that offer. The last thing I wanted was to have this conversation, but James weighed 300 pounds by now, and taking care of his needs by myself was no longer possible.

We arrived at the hospital. I had prayed all the way there that God, in His mercy, would give me words that would help James understand that it was the best decision and not just to get rid of him, though honestly, I was ready for that as well. But mostly, helping him in and out of the shower, out of the bed, and out of the chair was breaking me.

I stopped short as I walked into the room with Pastor Jason behind me. Pastor Jason asked me what was wrong. The noise I heard coming from the room had a familiar sound. I had recently listened to the sound of "death rales" or a "death rattle" in a video at school. The sound I heard coming from James' room sounded just like that. I didn't enter all the way in. I couldn't! My heart could not take this right now.

I got his nurse and explained what I heard. She smiled the all-knowing smile that said, "Oh, little nursing student, you don't even know what you are talking about." She told me she was just in there two minutes ago, and he was fine and talking. I asked her to check now, please. She followed me to the room, and I walked in behind her. As soon as she walked in and took one look at James, she turned to me and said, "It will be just a few minutes, and he will pass."

Less than thirty minutes ago, I left my mother's graveside. *This cannot be happening!* I remember thinking, *I am an orphan and a widow all on the same day.* I sat staring at the faceless picture on the wall. I had no thoughts—just a void where thoughts are usually formed. The noise stopped, and James was gone. *Am I supposed to feel relieved?* The terror of the past four years was over. But I didn't feel relieved. I didn't feel angry. I didn't feel lost. I didn't feel anything. No emotion.

Suddenly, I remembered two of my children were coming to the hospital to see their dad, and one of their friends was also coming. I jumped into action, telling the people in the room, and I don't remember who they were, apart from Pastor Jason. I remember saying, "Don't let them in here." Call them and stop them from coming. I will tell them when I get home. Unfortunately, I did not get the chance to tell them; others took care of that before I got home.

Three days after my mom was buried, we all stood again at the graveside. This time we were saying our goodbyes to dreams. Dreams of a life that could have been. Dreams of a life that should have been. A father that could have been loving and kind in his final years. A husband that could have considered someone as more valued or precious than himself. The hope for a future in which we would all walk with God with a common goal of seeing the Kingdom of God manifest in our lives and those we touch. It was all gone…. This week had been a week of dying to dreams. It was one of the most challenging weeks of my life.

As if that were not enough for one week, I got a call after I got home from the funeral. My nursing school was kicking me out because I had missed five days of school that week. Again, it was all just GONE.

Chapter Twenty-Seven
NURSING OBSTACLES

"I have made you and I will carry you;
I will sustain you and I will rescue you."
—Isaiah 46:4 NIV

"And all these blessings shall come upon you and overtake you, if you obey the voice of the LORD your God" (Deuteronomy 28:2 ESV). I must believe His promise. The seemingly unrelenting action of the nursing director to drop me like a hot potato from my nursing program left me numb. Yes, I had missed a week of school. I knew the rules, but was there no grace for extraordinary circumstances? As I spoke with her, she only recited the rules. However, several nursing school instructors fought for me, unbeknownst to me, and the director later overturned her decision to remove me. Praise the Lord. I don't know if that blow would have been fatal, but I was sure at the end of myself. It did, however, come with one caveat. I would need to take all three tests I missed that week and pass them on Monday before 9 a.m.

This news reached me late Friday night. The testing center at school was closed on the weekend. My response was to do what I had done all day. Cry! With so many reasons for tears, I couldn't say what triggered it this time. Relief? Fatigue? Fear? Anger? Hurt? Exhaustion? Everything about life felt overwhelming. With so much trauma in a single week, how was I supposed to study and get ready for any test, let alone three tests in under two hours when we commonly had one hour per test? The odds felt stacked against me, but I knew God had done great things already, and He was surely not done yet.

With this deep conviction to hold on to God's promise with everything in me, I turned my attention to my children, who, like me, were overwhelmed. Jenna needed me now. The other two children had gone off to others to seek solace. Jenna had come to me. She was overcome by all the loss, and she shed many tears. What she needed most was to be with me. She didn't need me to do or say much, but she needed a calming presence and an assurance that I was there. I had a chance to truly see her. For so long, access to me alone had been difficult to have with her father quick to interrupt our time together. This uninterrupted time provided a sense of peace and comfort for both of us. A few times, we held each other tight and cried together. For me, it was clear— studying could not be more important than this time with her. I did not open a single book that entire weekend. I could not have concentrated if I wanted to. We were all grieving. I was reminded of the scripture, "My grace is sufficient for you, for my power is made perfect in weakness" (2 Corinthians 12:9 NIV). Paul then says, "For when I am weak, then I am strong" (2 Corinthians 12:10 NIV). I knew His strength was the only thing I needed.

Monday at 7 a.m. when the testing center opened, I was standing ready with my two pencils. Before starting the test, I reminded the Lord, telling him out loud, just in case He had forgotten, "Lord, You have not brought me this far to drop me off on the curb. You will see me through. Your word promises You will not leave me, and I need You now. You are faithful, and I trust You, Lord!" One hour and ten minutes later, I emerged from the testing center with all three tests completed. I would not know my scores for a few hours, but I knew I had done well. I felt divine confidence like never before. Later that day, I knew I had experienced a miracle from God. Mighty God showed up, and I got an A on each test, and one was 100%. God was indeed showing off. I was able to complete my nursing degree just seven weeks later.

The next few weeks seemed to soothe some anguish as we moved from chaos to routine. The kids were out of school for the summer, but I still had to stay focused on school for my last semester. The four of us were moving on with our lives, coping the best way we could. I couldn't say there was a lot of joy, but there was a notable absence of anger. It was surreal to experience peace and loss at the same time. I suppose we had each gotten busy with life on some level and those activities helped mitigate some of the pain of grieving. Jenna became a new driver in those first weeks after her dad and grandmother died. For those with new drivers in their homes, you understand that teen drivers increase your internal angst on a scale like nothing else. What a thrilling experience, that is if you like drinking acid. My stomach churned and quaked in those initial days. Allowing and even encouraging your child to strap into the driver's seat of a 2,000-pound weapon is apparently necessary if you want them to grow. There is nothing fun or exciting, however, about handing your baby the keys to your car and saying, "Be careful honey, and be home by the time we talked about." It felt like a heavy cross to bear—especially during that season of life. But all in all, we were surviving, and our busy schedules made time pass quickly.

Before I knew it, eight weeks had passed since the dreadful week of loss. Graduation day from nursing school had arrived. Around thirty of my friends and family members attended my graduation ceremony to celebrate this mammoth accomplishment. They blessed me with their presence and loving words of encouragement. My classmates nominated me to speak at our graduation. It was indeed an honor. However, my emotions were on a speeding roller coaster, and fifteen minutes after I finished speaking and walked off the stage, I could not recall what I had said. It was as if I was watching the whole scene from outside my body.

After the ceremony, friends and family formed a receiving line, and they all lined up to congratulate me. It was wonderful having all my friends commemorate this moment with me, though a bit overwhelming. During the early months after the loss of Mom and

James, I was constantly on the verge of frantic emotions. God was so faithful to carry me through.

Four weeks after I graduated, I took and passed the State Board NCLEX exam to receive my RN license. I was offered the position I wanted with the Progressive Care Unit (PCU) at a local hospital. Even though I was super excited, I decided to delay my start date by ten weeks. I needed some downtime.

The first week during my ten-week break, Nancy and I headed to the Bahamas to veg in the most beautiful resort with a magnificent infinity pool next to the ocean. It was like a dream. Though I slept a lot, Nancy understood trauma had taken its toll, and she just continuously encouraged me that I needed to rest and recover, and whatever that looked like was okay with her. What a gift to have such a precious friend. It was a beautiful vacation.

Once I was back from the Bahamas, I decided to spend the next weeks off doing some remodeling of my home. Somehow, it felt so cathartic as I began my journey as a single person, considering my likes and dislikes apart from a husband. I would stare at paintings to consider if they were "my taste" or "our taste." I was going through a strange new separation. I had only six months of my life that I hadn't lived with my parents or husband. I chose to see this time as a blessing in my journey to self-discovery. I was learning to process the previous difficulties by doing something I enjoyed. One room in my house got many coats of paint when I was trying to figure out what color I liked. The whole remodeling experience was enlightening and enjoyable. Oddly, the constant sweat dripping from my face as I worked to exhaustion to create new from old was utterly fulfilling. Nobody required a conversation; I faced no demands except the ones I made for myself. I had no judgment, no criticism, no deadlines, and no complaints. I was restful in my soul even though I worked until I dropped.

Ten weeks blew by quickly, and it was time to start my career that I had worked so hard to train for. Never mind that I felt like something had died inside me, and I longed to stay sheltered in my home. Financial demands were upon me, and moving forward was the only way. On my first day as a nurse, I took a few moments to pray for wisdom and understanding, strength and focus, with a quick devotional, and I was out the door. I felt strong-ish. That is until day two of my brand-new nursing job. I had a patient with a Glioblastoma brain tumor, the same type of brain tumor James had.

Feeling confident I could be a support, I walked into his room, looking in his general direction, starting to say, "Hi, my name is Donna." We made eye contact as he turned toward me. Immediately, my breath caught, and I stopped short. I could have been looking at James' twin brother if he had a twin. The same size and physique were downright freakish. Feeling lightheaded and confused by the swirling emotions, I backed out of the room as if I had seen a ghost. Words failed me, and oxygen seemed in low supply as heavy darkness overtook me. My lips pinched tightly to keep the torrent of emotions from breaking free; immediately, I walked over to my manager. As I walked toward her, she lifted her head, and we made eye contact. With my chin quivering, I said, "I have to go home," and I walked away. I didn't wait for questions or a response. I offered no reason or explanation. I just headed straight for the elevator.

Alone on the elevator, pent-up grief, which I had previously kept myself from feeling or letting out, demanded acknowledgment. The elevator opened on the first floor, and I ran to my car. When I reached my sanctuary inside the vehicle, the tears flowed freely, my body was weak, my heart was pounding, and I was ultimately out of breath. A moaning sob from my gut came forth like a tidal wave for what seemed like an hour before I had enough of a release that I could get a forward motion. As soon as I could move, I called Nelson and shifted into drive. Thankfully, he answered. Through the deepest groaning of my soul that sometimes bordered on hysteria, I explained what had happened.

Nelson, always the voice of reason, did not comment on all I said; he only asked, "What is your plan?"

I thought for a moment and came to the only conclusion that made sense at the time… "I'm quitting!"

After a few quiet moments, Nelson asked, "What else can you do with your education?"

My heart was too heavy to think at that moment. I said, "I don't know."

He responded, "Perhaps you should go home, rest, and think about your path forward. Nelson reminded me how elated I was to get that position. It was uncommon then to hire new nurses in the critical care units, so I deemed it a gift from God and professed it widely to my friends.

Although his advice was always appreciated and most of the time followed, my emotional state was racing away on a path of its own. I hung up with Nelson and called the unit where I was working. The phone rang only once before it was answered, "PCU, this is Mary Jane; how may I help you?" Mary Jane McGill, director of nursing, happened to be on our unit when my call came, and she answered the phone. *How unlikely*, I thought, *that someone at her level would answer the phone.* That job was typically reserved for lower-level personnel. I had met Mary Jane at orientation, but I had not seen her in person during the two days I had worked in the unit.

Taken aback by this unlikely happenstance, I paused for a few seconds and said, "This is Donna, you don't know me because I just started, I just walked out, but I am calling to tell you I am quitting." She asked if we could talk about it. I responded, "No, sorry, I just need to quit."

I am confident she could hear my state because she took a moment before she asked, "How about next week? Can you come in next week, and we can talk about it?"

All I could say was, "I will try." She told me a time and a place and hoped I would come.

For the next two days, I did little but evaluate my life circumstances, wallow in self-pity, and try to figure out how I would have a job in a profession I now believed I could not do. How could I support my children and keep the lights on? It was the first time since my mom and husband died that I felt paralyzed. The forced demands and deadlines empowered me to keep moving forward. But here in this place, there were no immediate needs for my teenagers requiring my attention. There were no classes for me to attend. There were no tests for me to study for. All I had to do was go to work and produce an income. Why did that seem so hard?

I laid in bed for two solid days. I did have the sense to play Christian music, so at the very least, the presence and power of God's Word were in my environment. But honestly, I had never felt more alone in my entire life. I chalked it up to being without a husband and parents. I rationalized that anyone in my situation would be feeling the same things. I justified the darkness of my soul as being natural. But somewhere, deep inside, the darkness scared me.

I had never quit anything in my life, and I just went against all my nature and walked out of a job with no words, explanation, or caring about what they thought of it. *Wow! Who am I?* That was a scary place, indeed. But the Holy Spirit that dwells in me was still working to accomplish what He started. Though I had no conscious thought of the Holy Spirit, I knew that He was working, and I knew that Jesus was interceding before the Father on my behalf, as it states in John 17:22. How do I know that He was interceding for me? Because, in my soul's dark and desperate place, strength emerged, enabling me to begin to overcome the trial, acting with wisdom.

On Monday, I contacted an outpatient lab looking to hire. They asked me to come in on Tuesday for an interview. They offered me the job, but because I was not ready to commit, I asked if I could come and shadow a day and then decide. They thankfully agreed. I found out that I hated it! It was so dull. Take patient history. Start IV and fluids and wait. Send patients to the catheter lab, where the cardiologist would do the procedure. Then the patients were returned to me. They stayed with me until they were fully awake, and all bleeding was stopped. Then the IVs were removed, and they were discharged home. I did this repeat all day long. I was bored out of my mind. All I could think was, *if I have $40,000 of debt and have to do this for the rest of my life, kill me now, Lord.* I knew I was going to need more excitement and variety, which brings me back to why I chose to follow through with the meeting with the director of nursing at the job I initially thought was good for me but had just left.

On Thursday, I walked into the office and was greeted by Mary Jane and an HR person. Only then did I realize they thought someone had done something to me that caused me to leave. Over the next hour, I unfolded a tearful brief synopsis of the past few years of my life. They listened intently and were also tearful. But Mary Jane asked me why I chose to interview for the Progressive Care Unit. I told her that I had investigated where I would get the best education to become the competent, compassionate nurse I desired to be. She smiled the biggest smile and said, "I need you to tell me how we can make this work." I was perplexed. Did she want me back? I mean, I had just walked out and quit. She said, "Can you work eight hours a week? It would be best if you could work twelve hours because that is a full shift, but if you can only do eight, then eight it will be."

I don't know where Mary Jane McGill is today, but I can assure you that she is why I am the nurse I am today. In His wisdom, God had Mary Jane walk up to the unit near the precise phone with nobody else close enough to answer so she could intervene in my unbelievable world. She is undoubtedly why I stayed, grew in my confidence, and became an excellent nurse. The compassion she showed me, the grace she freely handed me—my mind is blown even now, more than twenty years later. I am not sure I have ever seen such care given to an employee—especially one that has been with the unit for only two days. But she empowered me with the idea that I may not be broken. I might need a little time after such significant loss. Indeed, she was right.

I continued counseling and made emotional strides, which translated to more confidence at work. Within a month, I was working full-time. Within a year, I was asked to cover for the nurse in charge on days when that person was out. That meant I was entrusted to be responsible for managing the whole unit of nurses and patients. What a change! I went from working part time to being called upon to fill in to be in charge when it was needed. All I knew was how much my life changed after God sent Mary Jane as an angel of hope. Of that, I am sure!

Chapter Twenty-Eight
FALLING INTO TEMPTATION

The trouble is not that I am single and likely to stay single,
but that I am lonely and likely to stay lonely.
—Charlotte Brontë

Work had become a source of life and hope. When I was there, I was capable and confident. But at home, I was lonely and weary. Before I went to nursing school, church was my life—maybe even my identity. But since I became a nurse, my schedule at work dictated my involvement in church, and I couldn't commit to many of the activities. It wasn't long before I learned a harsh truth; people forget you if you are not active in the festivities and gatherings at church. Nobody notices when you attend every other week and, for some reason, if you miss one of those weeks. I suppose the assumption is that you are at work. Unfortunately, that assumption makes it so easy for people to be absent for long periods of time. It also may prevent others from calling to see how the absent person is doing.

Being single was a challenge when all of my friends were married. It wasn't long before I was not invited over. I felt cut off. This isolation was one of the most significant blows to me. How easily they seemed to forget me. When I was the secretary and, in some respect, involved in every ministry offered at our church or through our church, I had friends coming out of the woodwork. But during this particular season, because I worked every other weekend and many Wednesday evenings, I couldn't be involved, nor could I spend as much time with others. Don't get me wrong, I knew everyone in the building, and we smiled, chatted, and hugged. I still, however, felt alone in the crowd at church. After the service, they went out to lunch with their families. I went home alone—to an empty house.

I felt broken, like I had some gross anomaly growing on the outside that didn't allow people to see me anymore. Therefore, church not only didn't nullify my loneliness, it enhanced the feeling of isolation. Perhaps it was all my fault? Honestly, it was because of this isolation at church that I began to feel sidetracked. The uncertainty of my place in these relationships weakened a crack in my foundation. During that season, I often thought, *Who am I? I am no longer a wife of twenty-three years. I am no longer a daughter to a mom and a dad. I am no longer a necessary part of these church people's lives. Who am I, and how do I cope?*

I did not want to give into those feelings. On those few occasions when I chose to join people at church, I still felt lost as a third wheel. I was single. Yuck. Not a word I liked, but it seemed less painful than "widow." The only widows in my church were my mother's age.

Still trying to walk in faith, I wondered if attending another church with a fresh start might be in order. That may be where I will find a good fit; one where I could meet widows still raising children. I needed some camaraderie.

I must say, however, it was a tough decision to leave my familiar church. Because everything was so up in the air, familiar seemed like an easier choice. However, I wanted to find someplace to belong, and this church didn't feel like I would ever belong again. I recognized that my desire to leave was all about my feelings. It was the place I dwelled in those days. I understood these people had walked with me through many traumas and tragedies. I knew I was uncomfortable in my own skin, and I did not blame anyone in the congregation.

I met with two of the pastors from my church. One was Pastor Jason, the senior pastor, and a friend. I had worked with him as church secretary for seven years, and during that time, we could nearly finish each other's sentences. I knew him. He knew me. So, I wasn't overly shocked that he wasn't happy about my decision. I was, however, shocked that he seemed angry.

Unfortunately, because of the trauma I experienced living with an angry husband, perceived anger caused me to shut down. It was the only way I found to cope. So, not surprisingly, my response was, "I'm done with this conversation; I have nothing more to say." I was sorry he could not be more supportive, but I loved him and thought he would come around.

I kept looking for a place to belong. A place where there were women like me, forty-something widows with children in their teens to early twenties. I know that seems rather specific, but that is what I was looking for. Several churches I visited made me laugh. I was amazed how many churches were filled with older people, a few very young people, but very few in the middle. I was speaking with a girl at work who recommended I sign up for e-Harmony, a Christian dating website. I considered it for a few months before I took the plunge.

I met Frank, a Christian leader in his church, or so he said. He worked in banking and seemed like a solid guy. After a few weeks of online chats, we agreed to go out on our first date, and I met him at his church. I loved the church. I met women like me, and I felt at home.

After a few fast and furious months with him, I was filled with regret. We began an intimate relationship that my sanctified heart would not let me enjoy. Guilt was eating at me. I talked with him about it, and he seemed to have excuses for why it was okay that, quite honestly, my flesh wanted to accept. Especially since many of the other dating singles in that church were also given over to their lust. The idea that worked in our minds to make our actions acceptable was that once you have tasted the apple, it is harder to say no. While this is true, my heart, or rather, the Holy Spirit, was working overtime to convince me to stop.

God's heart would float through my thoughts at some of the most inopportune times. Love does not dishonor and is not self-seeking (a paraphrase of 1 Corinthians 13:5). These were the very things I had taught to others in a more sanctified period of my life. I tried to justify my sin, telling God He knew I was not perfect. But I knew that was an excuse, not something God would applaud. An intimate relationship outside God's holy union does not bring peace and, therefore, cannot be from God. The flesh and spirit war continued.

I denied God's higher calling for several weeks, but it came at a great cost. I couldn't sleep, and I was being eaten alive by shame. I talked it over with Frank, thinking he would be supportive. Because we had read a devotional and prayed together, it seemed our relationship was not superficial, but he was not "feeling it." He had no guilt or shame. I struggled because I wanted him, but I wanted to stop being intimate. I suspected that I would have to make the hard choice. Even that thought seemed to yell at me, *If he cared about you, wouldn't he be willing to lay down his life or his flesh for you?* But the truth is, I had not been with anyone who had laid down his life for me. It was I that always laid down mine. I saw this. I knew this, and yet...

As the saying goes, the pastor got up and read my mail the following week at church. He preached how many in the church justified things God called sin. His first topic was intimacy apart from marriage. Frank was sitting at my side, holding my hand, listening intently. After the message, I cracked. No more lying. No more deception. It had to end. At lunch afterward, I told him straight. "I can no longer lie to myself, pretending God sanctions this relationship. I will no longer continue with an intimate relationship outside the marital union."

I felt sure he would be okay with it after that message so clearly drove home why we should not continue. The next words from his lips burned my soul, and I knew I had walked headlong into deception and eaten the fruit with a smile on my face. Without hesitation, he said, "I will not get married so I can have sex. Sorry, but we are over." Inhaling deeply to steady myself, I said nothing and pushed my chair back. With tears in my eyes, I walked away crestfallen.

As I walked away, I chided myself for being so stupid. Shame and guilt hung heavy on my soul. What did I expect? Sin never leads to righteousness. The truth was now glaringly obvious; he didn't love me. Love can't throw away a relationship that has been so close without any reluctance. It hurt me to the core. I was only a conquest, and the only feelings he had for me were between his legs. I was angry and hurt.

DRIVING AWAY FROM SIN

It was a typical day in late fall in Florida. Temperatures were mild, and the breeze was enough to enjoy a fall day. I should have been enjoying the drive with the open moonroof on my new Hyundai Sonata. It was blue with luxury seats. The speaker system produced glorious sounds that filled the car with grandeur. It drove like a large Buick but had the look of a Jaguar. I had a feeling of pride when driving that car, and it made me feel so good. Cruising with the roof open on such a day made me feel alive. But now as I was driving this beautiful car on this lovely tree-lined road that would typically bring joy and peace, those grand feelings were dust.

Why does life have to be so complicated? Why did I have to lose a husband? Why did I have to raise children on my own? And why am I now driving away from a man I knew I loved and thought loved me and God? My hands clenched on the steering wheel, trying not to grind my teeth, a problem I had developed with stress. Thoughts were racing through my head. He will see this was the best decision. I was chiding myself over the idea that I could allow such a man to remain in my life. But I did love him. Certainly, he will acknowledge that I was right. My mind was doing somersaults, trying to see the end. I imagined him calling me and asking for forgiveness.

Tears came harder, making the road difficult to see. Hopelessness filled every corner of my soul. I was such a fool. I knew better. Fear and loneliness were eating at me like hungry vultures. Depression was settling over my head like a black hood, and shame was the noose that threatened to suffocate me. Though I was driving along that beautiful row of lush green trees with the sun reflecting on me through the branches, I was a black cloud moving through light with no direction.

I desperately attempted to pull myself out of this dark place before I arrived home to my children, so I turned on the Christian radio station. Out of the darkness came light, and God put this song on the radio for me that day. I knew He was speaking to me on this darkest night with His truth. Casting Crowns song, "Who Am I" played and I could feel a deep stirring in my soul with every word.

I pulled off the road and collapsed in sobs so deep that I felt I might be sick. I was undone as the words of that song started to run down my soul like water on a filthy wall. I listened with my heart, and the tiniest spark of hope began. Closing my eyes, I tried to anchor myself to the truths of that song and stop the grievous thoughts. I am not a wretch, and I can be free of shame. I will make it. But inside, my soul felt like a graveyard of devastation, lost dreams, and hopelessness. I needed to listen repeatedly to that song so hope could be resurrected from the ash heap of my soul. I downloaded it from iTunes and listened to that song on repeat in my car ride home. My countenance improved and hope began to flicker even though my heart was still broken.

Sitting on my bed that night, I thought of how I was so easily entangled in this sin. *What is wrong with me that I let this happen? More importantly, I wanted it to happen. God help!* Denis Diderot, an eighteenth century French philosopher said, "We swallow greedily any lie that flatters us, but we sip only little by little at a truth we find bitter."[5] I found this quote to be the absolute truth during that season of my life. The lie that gave me what I wanted (attention) and felt I needed (companionship) was so easily swallowed. But when TRUTH was calling out to me, I shut it up for the lust of my flesh. God forgive me.

Chapter Twenty-Nine
THE PRISON DOORS SLAM SHUT

*Shame corrodes the very part of us that believes
we are capable of change.*
—Brené Brown

Saturday night came, and I was back in church, hoping Frank would be there to apologize. In my fantasy, he would see me and know that I was right. Purity in our relationship is worth the sacrifice. He would be willing to walk this journey. Suddenly, I spotted him coming in the back door with another girl on his arm, and I knew the truth. Their "relationship" was not new. They were far too comfortable to be newly acquainted, and the greater truth screamed in my soul…I was such a fool. I was gullible and drank of deception like a delicious drink, only now realizing it was poison.

Driving home along the same beautiful road as last week with the same feelings, I wanted a "do-over." I wanted to start life all over. I wanted a chance to make different choices and undo the decision to go out with Frank in the first place. Obviously, that was not possible. I wondered, *How do I pick up my life from here?* Hot tears began to cloud my vision. Fighting for control of my tears so I could see to drive, another thought hit me like a rocket. *What will my children think? I need to keep this a secret! If I tell people, I will lose every friend I have. Christians can be so unforgiving!*

Days passed, and I kept my pain to myself. At work, nobody knew I had a care in the world. I had such an ability to lock away my feelings when the situation called for it. My children knew something was wrong at home because I was quiet and stayed in my room, but they didn't question it. They just tried to steer clear. I felt trapped. But the pain was taking its toll and driving me into an abyss. Alcoholics Anonymous has a slogan, "You're only as sick as your secrets." I was living that truth. Shame hides in those secrets and blackens all of life. I knew the only way out was to confess. I had to come clean. I had to stop the poisonous thoughts, or this would grip me forever.

I continued to play "Who Am I" by Casting Crowns on repeat each morning, trying to renew my thoughts as I got ready for my day. Instead of a quick devotional reading, I started making Bible reading a part of my day, even if it was only a few verses. I needed to do something to get my soul back from hell. Some might wonder why I wasn't already doing this after I had been a Christian for so long. I suppose the short answer is that I lost my way, getting sidetracked. Nursing school, with the copious amounts of reading and studying had become all-consuming. I just stopped making the time. I lived in a state of being overwhelmed, and I lost my priorities. I let my feelings into the driver's seat, and I can tell you that feelings never take you to a refreshing destination.

The day came when I knew the truth had to come out. I decided to start with my children first who were now seventeen, twenty, and twenty-three years old. I needed to ask them to forgive me for lying and for the anger they had suffered from my bad moods. That was probably the hardest pill for me to swallow. I hated that they had to experience irritation from me. I had tried so hard to shield them from their father's anger, and now, here I was, stricken with the same disease. I didn't lash out, yell, or call them names, but I withdrew. I'm pretty sure one is not better than the other. In any case, I was genuinely broken over it.

One by one, I told each of them the truth. I talked about my shame and the destruction between me and my relationship with God. I told them that I was in a war to try to gain my soul, and if they learn nothing else from me, learn this. A physical relationship outside of marriage is not worth it. Fleshly desires will rob you of everything good and holy and leave you wanting for what you cannot have—peace! Only one child expressed disappointment in me with anger and disapproval. The other two were more worried about me than what I had done.

With the most painful confessions behind me, I moved on to my friends, Fran and Pastor Jason. I kept the lines of communication open with Pastor Jason for many months later, even after leaving his church, by calling every month or so. Admittedly, the last few calls seemed like he didn't have much time for me, but I still loved and respected him. And dare I say, I needed him. He had been my champion, and I needed someone to believe in me. Also, I felt Jason and Fran would always be family. Besides, I had not connected with any authority figure in my other church. Pastor Jason and Fran had been faithful friends and leaders. I trusted them.

The day to meet them arrived, and I was sick with fear but determined to follow through. The past three weeks since the end of the relationship had been the worst drain of energy, and frankly, the energy to keep up the facade was waning and starting to show other places besides home. I was a fraud, and I sinned against God. I needed to confess my sins to someone other than God. I desperately wanted freedom from this chain, so the time had to be right then. *How could this emotional drain be worse than confessing to people who love me?*

I arrived at church and was greeted by Fran. Fran was and is a forever friend, although we had lost touch since I had gone to another church. But I loved her, and I knew she loved me. I was so grateful she was there because she knew me. She knew I wasn't a loser. I just had a slip, and all would be forgiven and forgotten.

I went into the meeting with Pastor Jason and Fran. A million tears and a box of tissues later, my story was no longer a secret. The confession was over! I don't remember much about that day, but I still remember Pastor Jason's face when I told him I had been intimate with

Frank for several weeks. It was indeed a look of horror and disappointment.

He kept averting his eyes, not even wanting to look at me. He looked at Fran with disbelief on his face. I could read his thoughts. I had worked with him for so long; I knew all the faces of "Jason." Though surely not precisely as I am saying, his thoughts were along this line: *You are such a disappointment, Donna. Wow, what a joke that you have been in this church and ministered to the lost and broken, and you are more broken than all of them put together.* Then came the platitudes. "You know God forgives you of your sins. You know He died for all sins, and your sin is no different." Fran was sitting beside me now with her hand on my back. I believe she desperately tried to make me feel less alone or comfort me. I couldn't be sure because I could not take my eyes off Pastor Jason. I searched his eyes for forgiveness. But all I saw was judgment. I knew God had forgiven me. That would have to be enough. Pastor Jason could not hide his disappointment.

Chapter Thirty
GONE INTO HIDING

Once the heart gets heavy with pain, people don't cry;
they turn completely silent.
—Author unknown

The hurt I felt when I left Pastor Jason's office can only be described as life-altering. I didn't even have tears—just an ache where my heart had been. I don't know what I thought I would receive when I confessed, but I regret that day.

Rather than absolution, I felt condemned. I had always looked to him as a brother closer to me than my own blood. My thoughts were overwhelming. I just wanted to stop thinking about it. His face still looked away with shame every time I recalled that meeting. I wondered if maybe it was a little bit judgmental. Perhaps he thought, *I told you not to leave this church. That would not have happened if you had stayed here.*

Who am I kidding? I don't know what he was thinking; I only know I didn't feel good about the exchange when it was over.

Leaving his church may have been a wrong decision, or maybe I might have chosen to make the same mistakes even if I had still attended his church. I will never know. But I do know that I did not leave with any ill will. I felt like a fish out of water. My relationships at church had grown more and more distant. Mostly, people would say hi, ask how work was, and move on. I was no longer a part of the "in crowd." I loved my church family. It seemed nobody had known how to relate to me now as a single mother who no longer had spontaneity.

All things had to be scheduled, which was a challenge as my schedule rarely seemed to correspond with others.

I understood that I had changed. How could I not? The previous two years had brought an absurd number of traumas and resulting changes. Being single for the first time in twenty-three years can throw you for a loop. That, on top of losing my mom and starting a new career, undoubtedly resulted in dramatic changes in me. I suppose, given that the shifting in me was difficult for me to navigate, how much more so, for people who weren't living in my roller coaster world? Whatever the case, as I have said, church was hard. It no longer felt like home where I could be myself. I needed somewhere to belong, so I was drawn away. I did enjoy those new relationships and, unfortunately, fell into fornication. That is on me, and I get it. I guess I had really wanted a hug. I needed a person to say to me, "You messed up, but you are going to be okay." I wanted to feel like this mistake wasn't the end. I wanted to know that I was not alone.

Whatever the case, that meeting to confess my sins did nothing to help me. I was so filled with despair! All I could see was destruction. I had ruined my reputation. I was no longer the Christian leader, and my friend and pastor no longer loved me. Feeling so isolated, I questioned if I was even loved at all. *What can I do? Where should I go to recover? I have now been rejected by two pastors making me the common denominator. It is clear to me that I am the problem and worthless. This is all my fault. I should stay away from leaders. I must be the poison of these relationships.*

When I was attending church with Frank, I met Jan, and she and I became good friends. Jan was on several committees that served the communities around us. I joined her on many adventures, and I was beginning to feel my world being righted. Helping those in need brought true joy to my heart and a much-needed perspective shift. I loved that they had never known me and had no preconceived ideas about who I was. I was just Donna, the new girl that loves to serve people.

Chapter Thirty-One
TROUBLE AHEAD

There are wounds that never show on the body that are deeper
and more hurtful than anything that bleeds.
—Laurell K. Hamilton

As I continued to hang out with Jan, we did some very gratifying events. She had a gift for organization and was charged with organizing many community events, serving the underprivileged, and making a difference in the world.

One of my most memorable experiences was the year we did Angel Tree at the church. Angel Tree is a Prison Fellowship program that connects incarcerated moms and dads with their children at Christmas. The church makes a paper tree ornament for each child with a list that includes favorite colors, sizes, and other pertinent information. Before and after the church service, people peruse the angel ornaments to select which wishes they would like to fulfill. I was so emotional as we blessed these children in the Name of Jesus on behalf of their parents. As I participated, a precious gift was given to me—a piece of my heart began to reform. When we rang the doorbell and the child or children came to the door…wow, the look on their happy faces! They were greeted with "Merry Christmas" and a stack of presents with their names on the gifts. When we explained to the children that the gifts were from their parents, we were met with screams of joy, quizzical looks, and tears. Words fail to express all the emotions I felt. Many of the caregivers were grandparents, who would embrace us with gratitude and tears. Their grandbabies were gifted with hope. What a wonderful day to be alive and to be a small part of blessing others. Undeniably, it was a most memorable day.

Another project a couple of widows at the church worked on was a New Year's Eve singles dance at church. I was busy working, so I did not help organize the event. I did, however, agree to go with Jan. The event was designed to allow singles to meet other singles in a fun and safe environment. Jan was sick the night of the event, and I had no intention of going without her as I had sworn off men after Frank. But Jan talked me into it. She felt I needed to move on or risk getting stuck. Was it wisdom? Was I ready? I didn't know, but I had already bought the dress and prepared, so I decided to go alone.

The night was fun. Most people mingled with no serious thoughts of romance. I connected with a few girls sitting at a table. We spent the first hour getting to know one another, and I would have been content with just those encounters. But then, in walked Dean. Dean came and asked me to dance. He had a gentle spirit, and he was very sweet and gentlemanly. We danced most of the night. We talked. He was kind. I was far from smitten, but it was so nice to have someone pay attention to me and fuss over me. At ten o'clock that evening, I made my exit since I had to work the next day. Dean was walking me out, and I was so nervous that he would ask for my number. I debated internally about giving it to him.

Were these internal thoughts a siren warning of pending doom? Or was I just so vulnerable and afraid? I wasn't sure I wanted to meet a man at this point. I didn't want a relationship. They should have been a red flag, but I called Jan from the bathroom and told her what was happening. She said it was just a number, not a marriage proposal. That seemed like a reasonable idea amidst my scrambled thoughts. I decided to give him the number and hoped it wasn't a mistake. He called the next day, and I didn't answer because I was at work. I couldn't decide if I should call him back. *Why was I struggling so much? Was it God? Was it me?*

Though I wasn't sure what God said about going out with Dean, I was sure of two things. No man would get his physical desires met by me at the cost of my heart. Each time I was asked out, I announced that I didn't participate in sexual relations before marriage. It was amazing how quickly men professing to be Christians, would say goodbye before the first date. I understood that the desire for physical connection is intensely strong when you have already been married or in another long-term relationship. But I didn't care. I was not going through that again, even if it meant I would spend the rest of my life alone.

Second, I wanted to meet the people in a man's life if I was considering a relationship to discover what was truth and what was fiction about his life. If a man didn't want me to meet his family, church friends, and work friends, then there would be nothing to discuss. I would end it there.

So, when Dean called to ask me out, I agreed. On the first date, we had Chinese food and talked effortlessly. He asked questions and showed great interest in me. That was nice. When I told him there would be no sex, he was okay with that and even said, "I'm sorry that you have been hurt by men who didn't care for you the way they should." That was worth big bonus points.

The following months moved along with my planned inquisition of all things Dean. I visited his church, met his friends, and ate lunch with his coworkers. Dean had been at the same job for twenty-five years and attended the same church for ten years. He seemed stable, dependable, and well-liked. I even discussed medical history. I wanted to know all the medications he took and why. That is when I discovered Dean had had a schizophreniform episode in his early twenties.

My first thought was schizophrenia, which commonly happens at about age twenty-one. But he told me it was called Temporal Lobe Disorder. It was a red flag, so I told him I wanted to meet with his doctor before we continued the relationship. Fortunately, he had an annual appointment in the next few weeks, and he welcomed me to join him and ask whatever questions I had.

When I got home, I looked it up. Schizophreniform disorder is a mental health condition that has a limited duration. It has similar symptoms to schizophrenia but is usually a short-term condition lasting less than six months and can be controlled with medication. Schizophrenia is a serious psychiatric condition with severe symptoms and challenging to control, even with medications.

A few weeks later, we walked into his psychiatrist's office. The first time I had been in a psychiatrist's office, I thought it might look different from a regular doctor's office, with maybe a couch, a chaise lounge, and many plants for a warm, tell-me-all-your-secrets vibe. But it was very clinical, with a large mahogany simple desk and a comfortable chair for the doctor—a small credenza with some photos and two mildly comfortable chairs opposite the desk in a small room. We sat, Dean introduced me, and told the doctor to answer any questions I might have.

The doctor first asked his questions. "Dean, how have you been?"

"Great, no issues," Dean said in a matter-of-fact way. There were a few other informational questions, each receiving another equally positive response, "No issues." The doctor then listened with his stethoscope as the cursory exam of a psychiatrist. Then he asked if Dean had any questions, and Dean motioned for me to take the lead. I asked for an explanation of Dean's mental health.

The doctor flipped through the chart and read history notes for twenty years. His response was simple. Dean had been stabilized on the same medication for eighteen years. He had kept the same job and had no symptoms since taking the medication. I told the doctor we were in a relationship, and I asked if there should be any cautions I should have or take in this relationship. His response was no and no. Dean had been stable for so long that he expected that he would continue to remain so indefinitely. The doctor's information confirmed what I found. It was a short-term issue that would remain controlled with medication.

Dean came over a couple of nights a week. My children seemed to like him, and our evenings were lighthearted. Dean and I talked daily. He was encouraging and kind. We prayed together and attended church together. One day we were attending his church, and it was raining rather hard. Using an umbrella, we made it inside mostly dry. Once we were inside, he told me to meet him at Sunday School class, and he would be right back. He came in about fifteen minutes later, and he was drenched. The class had started, so I leaned over and whispered to him, "What happened?"

He smiled at me and said, "I'll tell you later." He told me what happened once church ended, and we were heading to lunch. When we were walking in, he had spotted a couple getting out of a handicap-fitted van without an umbrella. After he dropped me off, he went back and assisted them and allowed them to use the umbrella while he pushed the wheelchair and helped the couple inside. His kindness was evident daily. He never tried to get me to do the things that would shame me. He was honoring me and others around us.

Occasionally on the weekends, we would drive to the beach. We would sit in the glorious sun reading a book side by side. Love was blossoming. He enjoyed the quiet as I did. My first husband would never read a book. I tried so many times, and he would not do it. But here we were, quiet and content. We were reading separate books and sharing easy conversations about what we read. I was happy.

I took Dean to my former church one Sunday, where Jarred and Jenna still attended. Even though we rarely spoke, I wanted to introduce Dean to some of my old friends. As I introduced him, I consciously avoided my former pastor, Jason. I was not there to look at or talk to him. I was still clearly wounded. At some point after the service, Jason must have spoken with Dean because Jason came to me and told me Dean needed ministry. Was that a red flag sent to warn me? With my heart closed to all things from Jason, I never considered it for a moment. Several months later, I could tell the subject of marriage was on Dean's mind. I asked the Lord to keep me from a mistake.

Remembering the foreboding feeling, which I ignored about marrying James, I didn't want to repeat that trial. This time I needed a word. A few weeks passed, and I was preparing to leave for work. I heard a whisper in my heart. Hosea. I didn't recall much of Hosea's story except that God called him to marry a prostitute to reveal his redeeming love for Israel. As I pondered that, I was the prostitute in the story. So, does that make Dean Hosea? It seemed to make sense, and I knew I could use some redemption. I decided that when Dean asked, I would say yes.

Thirteen months after we met, we gathered at a beautiful location in Longwood, Florida. It was a cool night, but the warmth of the beautiful setting filled my soul. Twinkling lights lined the walkway and covered the gazebo where we would marry. Jan was inside, working feverishly to prepare all the food for the reception. The two instrumentalists tuned their violin and saxophone. It was a beautiful night to get married.

A truly inspired evening with heavenly music ushering me out the side door toward Dean. The sax and violin serenaded as I strolled to the center of the twinkling lights of the gazebo. Jesus was in this place. Our friends and family gathered to witness us exchanging our vows; the excitement was palpable on this perfect evening. Pastor Kent performed the ceremony, blessed our marriage, and the two became one.

Best of friends, life felt easy as we enjoyed the same things. Our off time was spent playing tennis, going on walks, and a day at the beach lounging with a good book. When he was at church, Dean was often helping someone with something. I saw what a servant he was. We had the usual spats, but our relationship was loving and kind. Dean liked to cook, making him a winner in my book. My idea of cooking was heating leftovers in the microwave. Life was good—until it wasn't.

Two years into our sweet marriage, we faced a life-changing challenge. Dean's dad, Alton, was a fit, retired museum curator. He was brilliant and kind. Unfortunately, he was diagnosed with Alzheimer's, and June, Alton's wife and Dean's mom, struggled to deal with their ten-acre farm alone. The farm was their retirement plan. They longed to live off the land as they had each grown up on farms. June, a retired nurse practitioner and mother of four sons and five grandchildren, was determined to handle everything. I understood her all too well. I loved her deeply and I was grateful for my relationship with her. It was especially nice to have a new mother figure in my life since my mom had made her journey to heaven eight years earlier.

One morning, June called with an urgent request. She asked us to come before Alton no longer recognized Dean. This was shocking as the diagnosis came less than six months earlier. It seemed he had declined absurdly fast. Fortunately, we both got the days off from work and were on a plane in less than a week. Landing in Arkansas at Little Rock Airport, I did not expect that Alton would recognize me as I was undoubtedly the new kid on the block, so to speak. We talked every few weeks by phone, but only twice in two years had we had personal contact. As Dean and I were coming down the escalator in the airport, they were waiting for us at the bottom. We waved, and they waved back. As soon as we stepped off, June embraced Dean, and Alton hugged me. He said, "It is so good to see you, Donna. How have you been?" Taken aback, I made eye contact with June. She shrugged her shoulders, showing she was as mystified as I.

During our week stay, Alton never seemed to have a "slip," as his mom called it. He was charming and made easy conversation. One night as I was helping in the kitchen, June whispered, "I know you have questions about what I said and what is happening." I nodded yes and said, "It is a little confusing." She responded, "I agree. Donna, last week he would forget to brush his teeth, refuse to shower, and forget appointments. Since you two have been here, he seems as normal as ever. I don't have an explanation."

After much discussion and observation, we determined that Alton was depressed, and the stimulation had rallied him. On the way home, Dean and I discussed the possible need to move to Arkansas to help with the farm. After a few weeks at home to pray and see how dramatically Alton changed back to the depressed person, we decided we needed to go forward with the transition to Arkansas.

TRANSITIONS

Four months later, we moved to Arkansas. Renting our house in Florida was a breeze. We found a lovely young couple, and they seemed eager to stay for a long while. That was a huge relief, especially since I bought a second house in Arkansas. The home was next door to Dean's parents but a quarter of a mile away. That is the way it is in country living.

Though we bought the house sight unseen, Dean's brother, Ron, had seen it and assured me it needed "lipstick and rouge." Let's say it was a gross misrepresentation of the facts. But it was ours now, and we needed to work through it.

When I received the pictures Dean's mom took on the closing day, I knew our work was cut out for us. Have you ever looked at a picture and just knew the smells of the environment would be putrid? That is what I knew. I had seen many renovations as my dad owned a construction company. Though I never helped him perform the work, I understood what was possible and what would need to happen with this home. I asked Dean's mom to hire a few people to start the work, so hopefully the house would be ready for us when we arrived five weeks later.

With our Florida home rented and our Arkansas home being readied, it was time to put in notice at our jobs and begin packing. Everything seemed to be moving without a hitch until the last week before we left. The storage POD was in the driveway, and it was time to load our belongings. Sunday morning, before I got ready for church for the last time in Florida, I walked into our bedroom and found Dean in a trance-like mode staring at the closet.

Admittedly, it raised a momentary concern, but once I called his name and he snapped out of it, it was over and didn't happen again. With the POD packed, the Florida home rented, and the jobs concluded, it was time to move to Arkansas. That wasn't a statement I would have ever thought I would make.

A funny fact was that when I told my friends I was moving to Arkansas, several asked where it was as if they were not sure if it was a state on the map. Though we laughed, I knew I was in for an adventure.

WELCOME TO ARKANSAS

When we arrived in Arkansas, we were excited to stop by and see our new home. Though it would be several weeks before we could move in, progress was happening. From the moment we walked in, I shifted from excitement to discouragement. Everything about this house was wrong, and I sensed way more hits coming before this house was livable.

After we had been living in Dean's parents' home for a few weeks, Dean was becoming easily angered. In fact, he had a temper that I had never seen before. I assumed it was because of the stress of our new money pit and not having our own private space to adjust. I wasn't exactly enjoying all these unplanned experiences myself. Living with others while navigating so many changes in your personal life is complicated. We each started new jobs in those first weeks, so life was overwhelming, and grace was needed.

Fortunately, the final wrap-ups occurred as the weeks passed, and we moved into our home; it felt almost magical. Having all our belongings sitting in the POD in our driveway, but not being able to unload anything lent itself to feeling there was no forward momentum. However, when the POD was empty, there was a palpable sigh in my spirit. Finally, we could get on with living.

The first year that we were there, we had some hiccups that gave me a reason to pause, but they seemed brief and random. For example, Dean got fired from his job. He explained that he wasn't fast enough. I knew the expectations of a pharmacy tech, and indeed, that job is very demanding. However, it seemed he was hiding something. I didn't get any additional insight about this thought, so I let it go.

I absolutely loved living in the country. We had only one acre, but we were surrounded by twenty acres, which included a small pond, some hills, and woods. Across the street was a farm with horses running in the field. It was beautiful and quiet. With the possible exception of skunk mating season, our property was a dream come true. On mornings when I did not have to work, I got my coffee and headed for the swing in the front yard. I played worship music on my phone and sang at the top of my lungs. Nobody could hear me, which was to their benefit. I read my Bible and took a walk. Being in the country was amazing, incredible, exciting, and freeing. I enjoyed working on the flowers, mowing, and some mild landscaping. It was very liberating and peaceful to be away from city living. I learned the importance of grocery lists because you wanted to avoid driving twenty-six miles round trip for a gallon of milk you forgot. With Dean, a few strange things randomly happened, but mostly I overlooked these instances and focused on how blessed I felt.

By the third year of marriage and after only one year in Arkansas, Dean's behavior was starting to be something that I could no longer ignore. My prayers for him were frequent and leaned more toward begging then a conversation of faith. Worry was creeping in as his weirdness increased. I discussed getting some counseling with Dean. He was uninterested as he said, "I know you think I'm crazy, but I am not. I don't need counseling. You do."

A foreboding feeling was ever present, and I was unclear how to react? *Am I in danger? Probably not.* He had tried to leave me in the dark on the side of the road miles from anywhere, but he had never hit me. By year four of marriage and two years in Arkansas, Dean was on his third job since we left Florida. He could not keep a job. I found myself perplexed. *How could this man be stable for twenty-five years in Florida and not here?* He was taking the same medicines he had been taking. I needed to get him to a psychiatrist to figure it out. His behavior was becoming suspicious and aggressive at work.

I spoke with our primary care doctor, who talked Dean into going to a psychologist. He did go for a couple of visits. Though I went with him, I don't know what happened because the psychologist would not let me in the room or tell me anything. But after two visits, Dean was done. He felt it was a waste of money. I was becoming more and more withdrawn. I was afraid to be around people for some reason. I felt like crumbling, and I thought I just needed to draw closer to God. What was happening, and what else could I do about it? I prayed constantly. I played worship in the house all the time when I was home. I read scripture to Dean when I was doing my quiet time. Slowly, he retreated from even that.

In May of that year, I graduated with my Master of Science in Nursing Education. I was excited to be able to teach at the university level. To celebrate this accomplishment, I booked a condo on Daytona Beach for Dean, me, and my three children for us to enjoy fantastic fun in the sun. Also, family and friends joined us while we were there to celebrate. While Dean's erratic behavior was becoming more noticeable, I prayed for this week to be a week of joy with family and friends and not one where Dean would get attention. God heard my prayer. There were a few abnormal things, but I could cover and shift the situation. Nobody seemed the wiser. Well, except for my friend Nancy. She picked up that things were a bit strained. I then told her I would talk about it but not right then. I was in constant warfare for normalcy. It didn't seem that anything could be done about it. Lord knows I had worked overtime, praying, thinking, pleading, trying to figure it out.

With a glorious week behind us, it was time to go home and return to regular life. The twelve-hour drive home was easy, and we shared some great time and laughter. I found myself hoping it would last. Maybe the break away from home was all he needed. But things were not better when we got home though not worse either.

Eventually, Dean started spending money on random things. I found this behavior a bit painful since he was not making any money. He had not worked in a while, and I was supporting him. I tried to talk with him about his spending, and his response was that this was our money. I agreed, but I added that this was our debt, and if you keep spending money and not contributing to the account, we would soon drown. I was becoming more and more frightened, not just because of his irrational behavior, but because I was going down financially. I had just lost my home in Florida in the market collapse. I had renters when we left Florida, but after the market collapsed and people could buy a house for half of what I was charging in rent, I could not get it rented. I had gone through savings trying to make it through, but ultimately, I lost the home I had for twenty-three years and had raised my children in. I still owed about $40,000 on the short sale. I was desperate and needed help. I continued to cry out to God. Help me walk in peace. Help me know You are there. Keep me safe. Let me know I am loved. I heard a song that ministered to me on a deep level, and I then played it—"The More I Seek You" by Kari Jobe—on repeat often. One line in the song would cause me to imagine my head laying on Jesus's chest and force myself to relax in His care. I didn't know what tomorrow held but I knew the future would drown me if I didn't hold tightly to Jesus.

I pleaded with Dean again to go back to counseling, but he was done with counseling because he didn't have a problem. He continued to point out regularly that I was the problem. He repeated that mantra each time I had "that look" on my face. The look that he referred to was a look that said, "Really? You believe that?" For example, one day, when we arrived home from church, he was angry that someone had come and killed a plant on the back patio. I "looked" at him with a question on my face. He said, "I know you think I'm crazy, but that plant was alive when we left this morning."

I spoke with the softest voice I could to not incite ire from him. "Dean, we live thirteen miles out in the country. Our closest neighbors are your parents and your brother. Do you think that someone would come here and destroy a plant and touch nothing else?" I guess I was thinking that logic would right the wrong in his thinking and stop the lunacy. But no.

Again, he yelled, "I'm not crazy! The plant was alive this morning." Since I was the one who took care of that plant, I can say with certainty that it was not alive that morning, but I let it go. This incident was similar to many other interesting ideas of Dean's that I had been letting go.

It was as if I could feel the ground quaking under my feet, and it seemed there was nothing I could do to stop being swallowed by the ground. I would give God my concerns repeatedly. In my journal, I wrote, "Whose report will you believe? Don't panic. Trust Him!" Panic, however, was a battle I fought moment by moment on most days…I read the Word, listened to the Word, and listened to online messages. A few days later, I wrote again in my journal, "Shackle those thoughts or they will shackle your life." I needed hope. I needed a lifeline. But what could I do about it? I had nobody but God. God had to be enough. I couldn't tell his parents because they had enough to deal with. I couldn't tell our friends because what would they think of Dean? I couldn't tell my friends because what would they think of me? And what could they do about it anyway? I was beginning to feel my world imploding. Honestly, isolation was almost worse than the shame of letting others in.

About a month later, I found out that Andrew Wommack, a Christian speaker and Bible teacher, was coming to Atlanta. I was elated as I knew that God uses him for deliverance. Dean knew I loved Andrew and agreed to attend the conference with me. I told Pastor Pat so he could agree in prayer for Dean to be set free. Freedom would mean he could hold a job and return to being the kindhearted person he had been. He suddenly became too tired at the conference to get out of bed. I pleaded with him. I prayed; I rebuked demons. I called Pastor Pat, and he convinced Dean to attend the conference. At the end of the first session, there was a prayer line to have Andrew pray for you. I sent Dean to get in line as I watched and prayed. Finally, standing before Andrew, my hopes were high, and my heart was racing. But the prayer was over before it seemed to get started. What had happened? I could feel the heat coming into my face and disappointment trying to overtake me. Dean returned to the seats, and I asked what had happened. He said Andrew didn't pray much.

WHAT? No more words than that. Not dissuaded, I dragged Dean back to the line and went with him.

When we got up to Andrew, I said that I wanted a prayer for him to be set free. Andrew said that just because someone needs freedom doesn't mean he or she wants it. He also mentioned that people must put in the work—or do their part—to be free. *Well, geez. Where did that leave us?* As we walked back to the seats, I felt lost. Angry. At whom exactly, I could not say. But angry! Or was it fear? Sometimes it was so hard to distinguish. Even though I knew what Andrew said was true, I had not previously considered that Dean did not want to be free.

In the weeks following, Dean started sleeping less and less. I again tried to get him help. I spoke with Pastor Pat, and he agreed to meet with him again. I prayed without ceasing. I got up each morning and put loud worship music on. I laid hands on the walls, bed, kitchen, everything and prayed against the spirit seeking Dean's destruction—our destruction. I started to sense that this evil spirit was lurking more often, but I would not give it freedom in my home. I would often see the shift in Dean's eyes, and I immediately spoke the name of Jesus. Either with scripture or just "Jesus, Jesus, Jesus, I love your name, Jesus." "You know what a blessing it is that Jesus loves us?" "Jesus, thank you for a blessed life," or I would hum, "Jesus loves me. This I know." It seemed to hold this evil at bay even though I was constantly aware that the war was real.

One morning I went into our room to wake Dean for work. He finally got his fourth job in four years because someone at our church vouched for him. I shook his shoulder lightly and said, "Hey, it is time to get up."

With a voice that did not seem his own, he growled at me with menacing words dripping in hate and contempt. He hissed, "What do you think you are doing?" His eyes were wild. His face was sinister. I had seen demons before, but never in my home.

I slapped his face and said, "Oh no, you don't! In the name of Jesus, leave."

Dean shook his head and blinked as if to clear his mind. Then he said in his normal voice, "Good morning, honey."

The chills swam over my body. *Get ready! Stay focused on Jesus and His blood!* I now knew the worst was still ahead, and only Jesus could bring protection in this home.

I spoke with Pastor Pat that day. I told him my suspicion that Dean had at least one demon was confirmed. Initially, he chuckled. I said, "No, I saw it." He was listening. After our conversation, he prayed for protection over us and for Dean to do what he needed to do to get free. I still had not told any other family or church members what was happening, including his parents. I believed that if I told people now, they would think I was crazy. I knew that people say that Christians can't be possessed and that they can only be oppressed. Whatever the case—possessed or oppressed—did not matter. I knew what had happened; it was as real as my breath. The influence of hell was winning the battle over the man sleeping in my bed.

Hopelessness was taking hold. I decided to come clean with Nancy. That conversation would take an additional book but suffice it to say, she was praying. I was so grateful to have someone in my corner, even if I fought constantly to believe there was a point to anything I had prayed for. I was angry at myself for being so stupid that I had gotten into this relationship in the first place. I was convinced that I missed God completely. He surely would never have told me to get into this relationship. I must have ignored the warnings because I was living in a nightmare. Most importantly, I was afraid for my life. His behavior was more and more erratic. He was increasingly aggressive with me. Dean never resorted to hitting me, but he manhandled or shoved me. All gentleness was gone. The Dean I had known was nowhere to be found. I started sleeping with my cellphone and my keys under my pillow, because the nights were the worst.

It was at this time that I confronted Dean about looking at pornography. He said he had only done it once and got there by accident. I explained that there is a little thing on the computer called "history" where I could see every site he had been on, and it was not an accident. It was a pattern. Whenever I was at work, he went on those sites. He insisted I was lying. At this point, I just wanted to walk out—to leave and never return. I was tired and broken.

Divorce is a dirty word in the church, and I was stuck. Besides, if I had heard God tell me to marry him as I thought I had, this was part of God's plan. I didn't want to jump ship before He calmed the storm. But it was damning to me to realize I was again in a marriage that felt like I was being tormented. Though both men were very different, the results were not so different at all. Daily conversations and prayers with Nancy helped me keep going.

One day when Dean was at work, I was praying, and God put on my heart to take the rifle from under the bed and hide it. I believed that the gun had to be hidden to protect Dean from himself. So, I took it to the guest room and stuck it in the back of the guest closet inside a solid white plastic bag that covered a gown. It was in such a place that I knew he would not accidentally find it. The nightly shenanigans had become more and more constant. I didn't follow him out the door, so I was unsure where he was going or what was happening.

Dean once again got fired. They cited some crazy behavior, and it all made him genuinely mystified. I remember being at his parents' house that night, and he told them what the employer said. His mom, always the voice of reason, said, "Dean, you had to have done something, or they wouldn't have fired you." He was angry, but he just got up and went home. She looked confused, but I suppose, on some level, she had also denied the increasingly weird behaviors. By this time, the crazy was my normal. I managed it with grace, and nobody was the wiser. I still had not mentioned to his parents what life was really like at our house.

One afternoon, I was out shopping for work shoes for my new job as a nurse practitioner when I received a text from Dean to come home quickly because I was needed. I had just pulled into the parking lot of the shoe store. I called and texted, but Dean had not answered. I began to think something had happened to his parents. I called their house, and there was no answer. I hopped in the car and made it home in record time. I was about four minutes from home when his mom returned my call. I asked her if there was a problem. She said no, they were outside with the new lambs. I told her what Dean's text message had said, and she did not know what he meant by it.

I pulled into the driveway and saw Dean standing in the doorway, leaning casually on the frame. Unbeknownst to me, the monster was there to take me out. I got out and asked what the emergency was. He said, "Nothing, I just wanted you home."

I was angry, and I wasn't afraid to say so. "Dean, I need new shoes for my work. You summoned me home, making me believe there was a problem."

He said, "There is a problem; I miss you and want you home."

I said, "Well, that is just great! Now I must drive back to town to get shoes, and I could have already bought them and been on my way home."

He shouted, "You don't need shoes. You need to stay home!" The evil in his eyes sent jolts of soul crushing terror.

Recognizing the shifting of his eyes and the contempt in the tone of his voice, I began easing my way back into the car. I said kindly, "I am going back to town to get some shoes, and I will be home as soon as I have them." He began to move toward me with a vicious sneer on his face. I jumped into the car, slammed the door shut, and shoved the car into reverse. Our driveway was a long curve, but one I had mastered over the years, thankfully. At that moment, I was in fight or flight mode. My heart was pounding out of my chest, and my ears were ringing.

I backed up quickly, and he jumped on the hood of my car and started pounding it with his fists, yelling, "Get back in the house." Once the car made the curve, he lost contact with the car, and I sped away. I called his mom immediately to tell her what had just happened. Dean texted me before I reached the end of the two miles to the main road. "What did you do with my rifle?"

I read the text out loud to his mom on the phone. I could hear the panic in her voice as she said, "Don't go back home."

Driving toward town, I felt hopeless. I realized that powerlessness is the moment you know you can't save someone from themselves. As much as I wanted to help, I now understood that help would have to come from another person.

Chapter Thirty-Two
GIVING UP OR GIVING IN?

Sometimes you have to give up on people.
Not because you don't care but because they don't.
—Anonymous

I quickly texted back to Dean, "I gave it away." I didn't want him to go looking for it. He texted back some unkind words, and I headed for town.

Tumultuous thoughts filled my head. *What now? Where do I go? What is the path forward? Can anyone advise me? Lord, help?* Regret was filling my heart. My sweet country, "forever home," was over. Even as I was driving away, I could feel my ideas of retiring in our quiet scenic country environment, enjoying sweet nights sitting side by side, under the stars, slipping away. My dream was dying. Just another dream in a list of other lost dreams. My life was upside down, sideways, and off the rails with no direction. My emotions were tumbling as if being churned under tumultuous ocean waves. I felt fear like I had never known it. Dread because I didn't know what to do, where to go, or how to proceed. My mind was stuck on the face of the wild man lying on the hood of my car, beating it with his fist and demanding that I stay home.

Driving the thirteen miles back to town, I only thought of being safe at our church. I needed some guidance and felt I might get it there, and equally important, most of the people in our church carried a gun. Though I had never cared about such things, I was profoundly grateful for those people now. I had never felt afraid for my life, but the fear was so terrible words cannot describe it.

When I arrived at the church, the parking lot was empty, and the church was locked. I first called a couple that were pillars in the church. Shockingly, when I asked if I could go to their home, I was told no. They don't get involved in that kind of trouble. Suddenly, I was stuck with the gravity of "this kind of trouble." What was I asking someone to do for me? Terror increased. "Lord, help me!"

Oxygen was harder to draw into my lungs. I was trying to grab hold of the Lord, but my faith was weak. I was drowning and feeling swept away, and my thoughts were not helping the situation. I was ashamed to be in this position. I took care of myself and didn't need people. The very thing I thought I heard God tell me to do was to marry Dean, who was now seeking to destroy me. *How could I be so stupid? When will I learn?* Once again, my life was being sidetracked by an event of epic proportion, and I was not sure how to respond. I felt like I wanted to wave the white flag on life and surrender. It was all just too much.

I forced myself to calm down and speak the truth of the Bible. "God, you will never leave or forsake me. Your plans for me are for good and not for evil. You will make a way where there seems to be no way. Your thoughts are toward me. You are good and kind and I will trust you."

Finally, I thought of calling Lori. She and her husband, Wade, had been small group leaders for me and Dean. I felt confident, though they had not said, they had to know, at least partly, some of what was happening with Dean. Lori picked up on the first ring. I quickly told her what happened and that I was at the church, but it was locked. She said, sit tight; I'm on my way. Less than ten minutes later, Lori and Wade pulled into the parking lot in separate vehicles.

Lori was the first to get to me. When she hugged me, heaving sobs came up from my core. Wade unlocked the church, and we went in and sat on the sofa in front of the fireplace. The place I often sat on freezing mornings before church. A place where I felt warm and comforted every time I was there. I could feel a genuine calm, trying to still my anxious heart. I unfolded the past four years for them. I could see them trying to fit in confusing pictures they had undoubtedly felt over those years. But they asked no questions. They listened intently and patiently as I continued. I told them everything I had done to try to get help for Dean.

Then they each sat on either side of me, I didn't know what would happen next, but I felt like someone was on my side. They prayed for God's wisdom and protection over the situation, and then Wade asked me what I wanted to do. I said, "I don't want to go back." It was agreed that I would call the police and get them to take me back to pick up my belongings, and then I would return to their home.

I followed the police officer's car back home and waited for him to check it out. Dean was absent. The police officer stood outside while I went in to collect my things. As I walked in, my emotions ran the gamut. *Am I giving up? Should I give up? God, where are you in this? Did I do something to cause this? What could I have done to stop this? Wait, this is my house. Dean never contributed any money toward it! He should be the one leaving! What can I do to make him go? I am so angry! I love Dean! Well, I don't love the monster taking over Dean. I don't love the...abuse? Wait, did I think the unthinkable? Abuse?*

More than a year earlier, Nancy had said I was acting like a battered woman. *Have I been and am I still? He has never hit me. But was it abuse when he got angry with me, pulled the car over to the side of the road in the dark, miles from anyone or anything, and told me to get out of the car? Was it abuse when he aggressively pulled me to the floor for his physical pleasure? Was it abuse when he consistently accused me of lying? Was it abuse when his behavior was so aggressive that my life was being lived out with fear of what might happen? Was it abuse that caused me to sleep with my keys and cell phone under my pillow? If he has a mental illness, is it still abuse?* It was all so confusing.

After a few minutes, the officer called from his post at the front of the house to see if I was okay. I said yes, I would be right out. I grabbed a few essentials, threw them in a bag, and headed for the door. On the way, I stopped and picked up the rifle the officer asked me to get. I thought he would take it with him, but he just wanted it away from Dean.

I put my things in my car and stood talking with the officer. I explained what had happened, and he gently responded, "I am sorry this is happening, but there is nothing you can do about it. Without evidence, and as a wife, it would be chalked up to domestic squabble." I asked about getting him committed. He said I would never be able to do that, as a wife, again for the same reason. I thanked the officer and drove away wholly powerless. All the prayers, proclamations, worship, and countless pleadings had been a waste. *What is the point? Why do I try? How was I in another hopeless situation? Help me, Lord!*

When I arrived at Wade and Lori's home, Wade assured me of my safety. Their home had an excellent alarm system; they both carried weapons and were unafraid to use them. This is not unusual in Arkansas. Finally, when I was, in bed, I lay lifeless in the safety of my friend's home for twelve hours. A cycle of sleeping, waking, and crying occurred on repeat throughout the night. *How did I mess up so badly that I am hiding? How did I miss God? Did I miss God? Surely God would not ask me to marry into this so I could experience such a tragedy. I felt so much despair, and the blackness of shame, fear, and despair settled into my soul. It resulted in utter hopelessness.*

During the next few days, it was decided that I should not return home. I called Dean and told him he had to leave the house. He understood, as he had not paid a single dollar for anything in or on that house since we had moved in. He left that day and moved into his mom and dad's house. When I spoke with June, she sounded as though she was trying with all her might to be understanding, but because I had not been honest with her, she didn't understand why I was being so dramatic. I knew I would have to sit down with her and clue her in, especially since she now had Dean living under her roof. But that would have to wait until my living situation got straightened out. I didn't want the house vacant, and because Josh felt they would be safe at my house, Josh and Jenna moved into my house, and I moved into their apartment. Dean wasn't a threat to the children; only me. I felt safer since Dean had no idea where Josh and Jenna's apartment was.

Hiding out in a tiny one-bedroom apartment felt less freeing than I thought, but I did feel safe from Dean. I was tucked away at the back of the apartment complex, and nobody would be there by accident. With minimal distractions, my days off were spent in reflection and prayer. Only a couple of weeks had passed, and the pain had only increased. I constantly ached to see things calm down and feel normal again. I think I knew that was not likely to happen based on the previous several years, but I found myself daydreaming of that glorious day. The Holy Spirit was coaching me to take my thoughts captive. In my journal entries, I wrote a quote from a book I had been reading and a few Bible verses:

> Don't panic—believe! If you indulge in panic, fear, anger, or hopelessness, it becomes a runaway horse that is hard to control. Once operating in emotions, it kills logic. You have a choice. You can be bitter or better. —Andrew Wommack, *Harnessing Your Emotions*

> So we do not lose heart. Though our outer self is wasting away, our inner self is being renewed day by day. For this light momentary affliction is preparing for us an eternal weight of glory beyond all comparison (2 Corinthians 4:16–17 ESV).

Admittedly, I was trying to remind myself that this was only a light affliction in the scheme of life and eternity. *Why did it feel like the end instead? Was I that weak?* I continued writing verses in my journal:

> So faith comes from hearing and hearing through the Word of Christ (Romans 10:17 ESV).

Therefore, take up the whole armor of God, that you may be able to withstand in the evil day, and having done all, to stand firm (Ephesians 6:13 ESV).

My self-talk was something like, "Okay, Donna, just focus on what you can do; eventually, you will get through. Immerse yourself in the Word." Or was that the Holy Spirit? I didn't know anymore. I knew I needed to cling to my only source of life. *Could I hear Him? Could I trust what I think I hear?*

My favorite verse from this period of my life was, "Jesus Christ is the same yesterday, today and forever" (Hebrews 13:8 NKJV). I loved this scripture for two reasons. I remembered a time in my life when Jesus was my first love. I knew I just had to repent, and He would be my first love again. But I was still frustrated when I repented of everything I could think of. I suppose I thought everything would change as soon as I repented. When it didn't, I thought: *What was wrong with my mind? Why would it not cooperate?*

However, the best reason for loving this verse was because I could think of all the people Jesus loved—people who were so undeserving of love by the world's standards. How about the woman caught in adultery? Wow. He who is without sin cast the first stone. Jesus taught so much in so few words. What I knew was that my life was a mess. But GOD! He is the redeemer of all the broken, used-up people. He will set my feet on solid ground. I needed to cling to Him. He would surely get me through. I mean, it had only been a few weeks. *Was I expecting a miracle?*

Dean did not know where I was living. However, he did know the clinic where I worked. Not surprisingly, he stopped by the clinic a couple of weeks after I left. Having explained my situation to my co-worker, she stayed in the office with me while Dean was there. My guard was up, and I felt anxious, but I was thankful for her presence. Not that I wanted people to know what state my life was in, but I was past the point of protecting myself or Dean.

Dean wanted to know why I left. Honestly, it was perplexing even to be asked the question. I told him he scared me, and I could no longer live with him. Oddly, he said he was sorry and asked if there was anything he could do for me. I said, "Well, now that you mentioned it, you could go to the house and collect your belongings." He still had that distant and dark look in his eyes. But he was calm and agreed. *Thank you, Lord.*

The moment Dean left; a familiar pattern of thought returned. *What am I afraid of? Dean had been calm and caring. The Holy Spirit protected me. I could go back. The Holy Spirit can defeat this evil, and I could have Dean back.* When I got home to my little apartment, I wept tears of confusion, hurt, abandonment, and hopelessness. I felt broken while trying to console my heart with truth from God's Word. It always came back to the years I have lived with the undercurrent of fear in my daily life. Sometimes when I closed my eyes at night, I felt that familiar need to grab my keys and cell phone. When would this pattern reverse?

I had lunch with June a few days later when I learned of a greater tragedy. When I initially told Dean's parents about the nightmare I had been living, they found it hard to believe. They didn't say that, but I could see the skepticism on their faces. Sadly, I learned they had experienced an event that convinced them that the psychotic break was real. Perhaps one of the greatest tragedies of this experience was the hurt caused to his mom and dad.

Dean acted irrationally after only a few days of living in their home. June, attempting to center him with the Word of God, opened her Bible, which awakened the demons. He gritted his teeth and snarled something at her, grabbed her Bible, threw it to the floor, and grabbed her hard enough to leave bruises on her arm and soul. He terrified her and his father. They stood watching him in complete shock. Until that moment, they had never seen this kind of evil in Dean. Sure, they saw plenty of times of pure delusion or irregular behaviors. But nothing on this scale. June told me that Alton told her if this is a taste of what Donna has been living with, I don't know how she has made it this long. As sad as it was to hear, somehow, it made me feel validated.

They saw what I knew, and they believed. June said they called the police to report the abuse of their adult son on his mother. The police came and picked him up but returned him to their home several hours later. His dad met him at the door and told him he could not come in. He would not be welcome there until he agreed to see a doctor. And he chose not to seek help. Mental illness can destroy everyone and everything in its path. The unknowns are overwhelming. Dean was now homeless, squatting in an empty home, and June's hurt was palpable. It was all so terrible.

I held out hope that perhaps Dean would wake up to the reality that he needed help. Maybe the right person would say something to persuade him since everyone in our small town seemed to know our personal nightmare.

During the next two months, as if it was an answer to the questions swirling in my head, Dean was living on the street and fully engulfed with demons. He had acquired several restraining orders from various businesses around town. Sunday at church, I would receive the weekly "Dean sightings," as I called them. Many would come to me and tell me where they had seen Dean that week.

"I saw Dean standing in the middle of the street with a gallon of water and a stack of cups offering a drink to those who passed by."

"I saw Dean at Taco Bell being escorted out. I don't know what happened, but the manager was angry." On and on, week after week, there was no question that the secret was out. Everyone I knew and people I didn't know were fully aware of the details of my personal life.

Suddenly, word around town was that Dean had purchased several vehicles and wrecked two. HOW, I wondered? He had no job. This information started to freak me out a little. I looked on Google and picked an attorney based on his solid name that seemed to register with me, hoping I heard God this time. My trust in my ability to hear God was shaky at best, but I had no other options. I made an appointment with an attorney to figure out how to file for separation so Dean could not put me further in debt.

The next morning, spilling my story of the past seven years to two attorneys and using nearly a whole box of tissues, the lead attorney said, "I can tell you are a woman of great faith."

I thought, *Ha. Faith...I think not but go on.*

He continued, "Do you think God has called you to stay in a relationship that causes you such fear? I know God has good plans for your life." I listened, wanting to believe I hadn't wrecked all of God's plans for my life. He kept going, "It will cost you the same amount of money to get a separation or a divorce. The difference is that the separation is temporary, and the divorce is final. Also, the separation will not absolve you of debt that he can still create in both names. I need you to pray and consider what you should do. But if you ask me, you have been faithful. You have prayed and given up life to help this man get the help he needs, but he will not choose the help. Doesn't God do the same? He offers us help, but if we choose not to accept it, we are released to our own desires." I was too emotional to make such a decision. I left that day agreeing to think about it. He told me everything I would need to do to keep my home and what would be necessary to get an uncontested divorce.

I discussed my options at great length with Nancy on the way home. She listened and prayed. She said, "Donna, I know you will hear from God." *Why did she have the confidence that I would hear from God? Was that just a cliché answer? Hadn't I believed I was listening to God when I got into this mess? Doesn't that establish that I don't hear God well?*

I got home and wept. I asked God to make it clear. "Show me in a tangible way that it all makes sense. I am tired and worn out. I don't know anything anymore. You, Lord, must do what only You can do. Reach past my emotions and cause me to know your voice."

A few weeks later, I was in church one Sunday, when George, one of the security personnel at church, came to get me out of the service. He whispered, "Dean is in the lobby. Come with me." Dean wanted to go in and worship. They would not let him in, but they wondered if I would come out and talk with him. Glad not to be alone, George walked with me to the welcome area where I was to meet him. Seated at one of the tables with another security person was a man who resembled the man I was married to. This man was unkempt in every sense of the word. He looked as if he had not shaved, bathed, or brushed his teeth in as many months as he had been gone. He was truly emaciated as well. I sat at the table in the coffee reception area with Dean, an armed security person, and a deacon to have a "private" conversation with Dean.

Dear Jesus, is this what my life has come to? While I was thankful for the protection, I was truly humiliated. It was all too much. The security person was a sweet, godly, older father figure who was gentle and kind to Dean. I asked Dean what he wanted, and he said that he wanted to come home.

Spine-tingling shivers went down my back at his response. Drawing confidence from his parents' stance, my resolute was unbending. "Once you have gotten help." I saw immediately in his eyes that there was no belief that he needed help. "You will never be invited back into my home without treatment." He didn't speak and stood to leave. I think I had my answer. He would never be willing. Help would only come when it was imposed.

I thought of the thousands of times the Holy Spirit had woken me to lay my hands on Dean's sleeping body and pray for a sound mind and a right heart, for angels to dwell there and to help me set a guard over my heart. I recalled the countless times I had stuck words to worship songs in his hands and had him sing with me songs that declared Jesus is Lord. I had spoken the name of Jesus millions of times when I was afraid. In the days that followed Dean leaving my home, it became clear that the Holy Spirit had more than one reason to wake me in the night. My Holy Father protected me from the chaos of Dean's mind. He rescued me from the demons now unleashed on Dean.

I loved the Lord and thanked him daily for His protection and covering. But the concern that I may have brought this on myself still ate at my soul like necrotizing fasciitis eats flesh. Necrotizing fasciitis is a rare bacterium that spreads so quickly that, if not managed expediently can result in loss of limbs, loss of organs, or even death. I felt I needed to do something to squelch the rapid destruction of my thoughts, but I was empty of ideas for how. I still prayed and worshiped my heavenly Father, but shame blocked me from intimacy with God. I also had no real lasting hope or ability to overcome my anxiety and questions.

How could I possibly have heard God? God did not tell me to marry this man. Would God risk my life for this man? How can I believe that the God who saved me from eternal death and literal earthly death in this relationship would want me to go through this? The darkness was so great.

I desperately wanted to disappear. Life seemed too hard. I wanted to run away from all people. I wanted to get a fresh start and a chance to reinvent myself. I needed to stop remembering the trauma that I thought I had caused. But in the most authentic style of a child raised by a Marine, I continued to work and smile as if all was well in my world.

I would find myself daydreaming about this place called "FRESH START." Though I was "fresh" out of ideas on how to go about it, the dream was genuine. It didn't bring life to my soul as much as it brought hope that there could still be life there. I felt void of direction, a cause, or care.

Having my entire community privy to the ghastly details of my life did not help. Their care felt more like curiosity than genuine care. *Were they really interested in discovering how this seemingly confident nurse practitioner could end up in this dreadful place?* Or was that my question and mine alone? *Maybe they did care? Geez, I just needed a fresh start! A chance to reinvent myself and become someone not known by the chaos of my life.* A fresh start would give me a chance to develop relationships with people who didn't know the most intimate details of my life.

Author Joyce Meyer advises people to "think about what you are thinking about."[6] I did just that. *Was this starting over a practical thought? If I could have a fresh start, where would I start? Before I met Dean? Or perhaps before I got married the first time? Or perhaps when I didn't bother to tell my Sunday School teacher in the sixth grade that I didn't know Jesus because I didn't want to go to the little room with someone to talk with me? What if I had been brave? Could my life look different now? If one wishes for a fresh start, what exactly do they wish for? Alaska?*

Funny that Alaska had always been in my mind as a place to escape to. Truthfully, I don't think this Florida girl could survive the cold. I hibernate when cold weather comes and only come out in warmer weather. I am like a flower. I start to awaken in spring, and the summer is my most excellent luster. Fall brings a little wilting, and winter puts me under covers to protect myself from frostbite.

With a move to a new place seemingly off the table for practical reasons, it was time to focus on getting God's perspective on the rubble of my life. Whatever happened would affect my future, and of that, I was sure. But I knew in my heart that it could have a positive or negative effect, depending on my response.

After all, the Bible tells of people making foolish decisions that did not result in complete failure. King David committed many sins. 2 Samuel 11 and 12 tells of his exploits in coveting, adultery, and murder. However, after he repented, his failure was not terminal. Sure, he had consequences as a result of those poor choices. *Don't we all?* But, in Hebrews we read about David and several other people in the Old Testament:

> By faith these people overthrew kingdoms, ruled with justice, and received what God had promised them. They shut the mouths of lions, quenched the flames of fire, and escaped death by the edge of the sword. **Their weakness was turned to strength. They became strong in battle** and put whole armies to flight. Women received their loved ones back again from death (Hebrews 11:33–35 NLT, bold emphasis added).

The bold part of these verses gave me hope. I desperately wanted to see something positive come from my circumstances. I knew I had to fully surrender to the Lord to unravel this tangled mess I called my life. I started first by repenting for trying to do life alone. I needed

Him. I was unsure how to proceed but asking Him to forgive me was as natural as breathing. My next step was thanking Him for His incredible protection.

The prospects forward seemed daunting. I no longer had any God-confidence. Not because of God's abilities, I had never doubted those—I had only doubted my abilities to hear Him! Thinking about making such a colossal mistake that would have lasting consequences nearly paralyzed me. However, I still had TRUTH. Somewhere in my soul TRUTH was calling to me. I could feel it. If I could lean into God, He would get me past this cave of darkness that was trying to suck me into its depths. I had seen Him rescue me so many times, and I knew that if I would not get sidetracked and instead surrender to get myself out of the way, He would do it again. It was exhausting work, and I fought hard to escape fear, guilt, shame, and anxiety.

Chapter Thirty-Three

HOPE FOUND IN PURITY AND INNOCENCE

Gifts come in all forms.
We need only to open our hearts to see them.
—*Donna Bess*

Though I was still under such a weight of trauma and terror, I had a glimmer of excitement on the horizon. We all know the saying that God's timing is perfect. Indeed, it is. Though I could never have guessed that I would be hiding away from my husband and the hurt that was felt so deeply, I also could not have imagined that God would have chosen this time to give me a gift. Oh, what a great gift it was and is.

On July 26, 2013, just five weeks after I fled my home to the safety of this little apartment, my life changed forever. Purity and innocence came into my life. Perhaps one of the greatest joys I have experienced in my adult life, God provided this precious gift for such a time as this. This gift took me from hopelessness to hope, from no direction to a precise knowing of my path, at least partly. This gift was the lifeline my precious Savior knew would build the bridge in my heart to healing.

Purity and innocence came in the form of a tiny six-pound package that captured my heart. Her name is Lily Grace, which means purity and innocence. She is my first grandchild. This tiny little person had the remarkable ability to bring light and joy into the room. Though my relationship with her mom and dad was strained at the time over some hurts, Lily was a source of joy that brought all three of us to some common ground.

Her mama and I shopped for the perfect crib bedding set in the weeks before her birth. As if Mama knew her sweet baby girl would love animals of every size, color, and shape, just like herself, she picked the most adorable pink set with a giraffe, zebra, monkey, elephant, and cow against the softest pink print that was perfect for the innocent life that would occupy that space in her earliest days.

In those special weeks before Lily's birth, my sweet daughter, Jenna, and my son-in-love, Josh, and myself, prepared the home space and our hearts. Painting and decorating the room brought joy and a remembrance of a much simpler time of life when I was a new mom. It filled the emptiness inside me. I found a picture of Jenna when she was about eighteen months old, along with a picture of her dad and me when we were that age, and I hung them on the wall in the nursery. I was excited to create an environment that looked perfect for this precious little one that would one day call me Nana.

As this precious new life lie snuggled, sleeping peacefully in her perfect girly animal-filled room, I, as Nana, found new life and a reason to be, love, and smile again. I wanted to be with her when I was off work, so I always offered to be with her. Being there was not without a struggle.

Carrying a baby and all their paraphernalia is much easier when we are young. At fifty-four years old and not in the best shape, carrying her and her stuff wore me out, but didn't hinder my desire to continue. I was all in for any time I could watch her. I rocked her, sang to her, and prayed for her constantly. I received as much care from holding her as I gave her in her early days. I was grateful to be blessed to have her in my life. She was indeed a lifeline. As I was sitting quietly with her, I could feel healing taking place in my heart.

Although Lily was a piece of Heaven gracing us on Earth, Dean continued his dive deep into an abyss. The number of restraining orders continued to mount up. I was at a loss about making decisions. I didn't want to give up on our marriage. I didn't want to give up on Dean. Though I didn't know the person he had become now, a wonderful man was still trapped inside. I went back and forth in my mind.

One day, I had my daily telephone lifeline connection with my sweet and faithful friend, Nancy. She asked a question that shook me into reality. She asked, "If this was Jenna (my youngest daughter), and she had to make this decision, what would you tell her to do?"

My first and only thought was to say, "Run for your life." Right or wrong, my decision was made. I contacted the attorney and paid the fee for the divorce.

I needed to have a document signed and notarized by Dean to keep my home, and I also needed Dean to sign the uncontested divorce document. Obtaining these signatures would be a miracle since Dean was rarely of sound mind these days. Conversation with him was difficult. I continued to pray that if it were God's will for me to get divorced, He would make it easy. One day I was coming home from town when his mom called me. She said, "Donna, Dean is at my house. He seems as stable as I have seen him in months. Take your document over and get him to sign it."

I drove to her house, and Dean was standing in the driveway. He looked a little better than I had seen him in the several times he stopped by the clinic. He had bathed but was still very scruffy and emaciated in appearance. When he saw me, he said, "Hi, friend! What can I do for you?"

The chills can still be felt in my spine when I think about the eyes looking at me that day. I smiled back and asked if I could talk with him briefly. With a genuine, although disinterested smile, he said, "Come in." I say disinterested because it felt like an exchange of near strangers instead of a married couple. Unsure how to proceed, I went to the porch and sat on the rocker. Going inside the house behind a closed door with nobody else home at the time seemed unnerving.

As if we were enjoying the beautiful sky and chatting over coffee, I casually asked him if he would be willing to sign my house over to me. He said, "Sure, it is your house." Then I asked if he would be willing to sign divorce documents. He said, "Yes, you are my friend." I told him he would need to meet me at the bank at 1 p.m. that day to get the papers notarized. He said he would be there.

I rose to leave, and he stood. For a moment, I was afraid he would try to hug me or touch me, but he didn't. He just stood there smiling the strangest, weird smile. My mind flashed back to the demon screaming at me and beating the hood of my car. Shivers covered me! I walked back to my car, mindful of every sound of the gravel under my feet, careful to listen for the possible footsteps of him following me to the car, but there were none. I turned to sit in the car, shaking. I looked, and he was still standing where I left him with the creepiest smile. I started the car and drove away. I could not get the foreboding feeling to leave me. I had dealt with completely unstable and unpredictable for so long that I was prepared for anything to happen. But nothing did.

I went home, got all the paperwork I needed signed, and headed back to town. I called Nancy and my pastor and asked them to pray that Dean would show up and that there would not be a scene at the bank. At 1 p.m., I was sitting in the bank lobby when Dean walked through the door. They called us back to the woman who would notarize the papers, and in a matter of ten minutes, it was done. All paperwork was signed and notarized. I thanked Dean and wished him well. No drama, no complaints, and hardly any conversation. Just finished. Final. No matter how I look at it, seven and a half years, ninety months, or 2,674 days marked such a short yet dramatic time.

Trying to process this finality, I drove thirty-five miles straight to the attorney's office to turn in the documents. I received the notarized copy of the final uncontested divorce decree about a month later. I have heard women everywhere say, "I am finally free." They celebrate with friends and see it as a golden ticket. It may sound unbelievable, but I still did not feel free. My emotions felt as dark and unsure as before I signed the papers.

I was no freer than I was the day he jumped on my car and hissed, "Come back in the house," as he pounded on the hood. I was utterly unnerved by him.

Sadly, Dean continued to travel down a very dark hole. The few days he was of sound mind were short-lived, and he was back on the street. He had taken up residence in a man's home that had hired him to work on one of his rentals. He told us the man was allowing him to stay there. We later learned that Dean, seeing nobody there, decided to squat there. It took a couple of months before the owner realized this unfortunate news, and he had to take legal action to get Dean out. More than sixteen restraining orders were filed in our small town against Dean. Dean was not allowed into many places, and ultimately, he returned to one of those places. It was a Boys and Girls Club, making it a federal offense. Dean was arrested.

I was let out of self-imposed protective custody with Dean safely locked away. I was uncertain what would happen to Dean, so I cautiously proceeded. After six months, we learned that the psychological evaluation had determined he was unstable and remanded him to a state psych facility with a mandatory five-year minimum.

It was a long and trying time for everyone involved, and it was incredibly taxing on his parents. I cannot imagine the pain and suffering they endured while Dean went weeks with no contact and no knowledge that he was okay. But now, finally, Dean was safe. He would be forced to receive help, and he was no longer living aimlessly on the streets. Though it was not what they would have chosen, Dean was no longer at risk for much worse trauma.

With the divorce final and Dean being remanded to a psych facility, I was filled with strange emotions. What does a person do when all of life has been shaken? I was relieved to sleep without having to rehearse scriptures to quiet my soul. I was happy to be able to be back in my home and not feel I needed to be on high alert. But mostly, I was sad to my core.

The sadness was a cloak of darkness that I didn't know how to rid myself of. I knew God was with me. That was so apparent, especially in the days after I asked Dean to leave. When I saw what happened to Dean outside of the constant prayer covering and anointing, and the fact that I had had him in my home, I was highly aware of the protection my Heavenly Father brought me and my family. So, how could I be so fully aware of the presence and protection of my Almighty Father and feel so defeated and destroyed simultaneously? This question is one that would take me years to unpack. But in the meantime, there was Lily.

The cares of this season were softened by my love and desire to share my space and my heart with Lily. My love relationship with that child opened my heart to forgiveness—not just toward Dean but also toward myself. The questions remained, but I could accept that regardless of whether or not I heard God tell me to marry Dean, God was so faithful to love and protect me, and I would be okay moving forward.

Despite the healing, there was restlessness in me. I didn't want to stay all alone in the country. I didn't want to stay in this home; the home that I had poured so much money into to create a warm and inviting home. The idea of it being my forever home no longer held the promises it once had. I wanted to move away. I needed to move away from the memories and trauma. *Where? When?*

I listened to messages from various pastors and teachers in my free time. I played worship music all the time. I prayed for wisdom. All I could hear was..."Be still and know that I am God" (Psalm 46:10 NIV). And in case I forgot that message, that verse was on a wall decoration I won at a women's function. God was serious about me just being still. I sought the Lord like a man dying of thirst in the desert. But intimacy with my Father seemed a thing of the past; I didn't know how to get it back. I cried out for Him to teach me and to not let me do any more dreadful things with my life.

After many months, I felt it would be best to sell my house and move. It took several months to get the house ready, but finally, I put it on the market. I quickly learned that people only move to the country for acreage. My one acre was too small for most that looked. The offers were much lower than even what I had in the house. After many months of praying and believing for more, I sold at less than I had hoped, but more than the first offers.

With the house sold for less than I had put into it, it felt like another failure. At church, I wanted to sit in the back and lick my wounds, so to speak. I hate pity parties and I don't care for people that are always having them. It follows that I didn't like myself because I was living a bit of a pity party, and therefore, I didn't want to interact with others. I had nothing to say that would edify anyone. So, I had nothing to offer.

As for the people in the church, I have learned that when your life presents you with challenges that others know nothing about, their lack of comfort can look like a lack of care as they avoid you. It isn't their fault. They don't know what to say. I was miserable and tired.

Chapter Thirty-Four
CHURCH PLANT

Not all storms come to disrupt your life,
some come to clear your path.
—Author unknown

Josh and Jenna had moved to the beautiful mountains of Colorado with my sweet Lily. They went to help a pastor, who Jenna had met in Bible college, plant a church. Their hope since they got married was to be in full-time ministry, so they were so excited. I wanted to support their passion and chose to help them financially as they got started.

At the time of their move, I was again reeling from another painful situation that left me in probably one of the most devastated places I can remember. I cared for a patient that I felt should be admitted to the ICU. However, the powers over me felt different. Instead of being admitted, the patient was discharged. Admittedly, the patient wanted to leave. However, the following day, that same patient was found dead. I was destroyed.

Though I was never held responsible, I mourned. I was grieving because my opinion was not valued. I suffered because my confidence was too weak to stand up for what I felt in my gut. I was grieving because a life was gone, and I might have missed the opportunity to change that if I had had more courage to fight harder. I groaned in the fetal position in my bed for many days, trying to process this loss. I prayed for relief from this pain, but I could not find it.

One morning, I awakened to numbness. No more tears, no more grieving. Just empty. I needed to move on. It was time. I returned to work, but half my heart was gone. I had so many questions that remained unanswered. This loss took me down to my knees.

One night as I was speaking with Josh and Jenna, they asked me to pray about coming to Colorado to help care for Lily while they worked and did ministry. I didn't really pray. I used two key words: "Help" and "Lily." I was desperate to be with Lily. For a moment, I wondered if I was making a mistake, given the state of my heart. My past relationship with Josh and Jenna had not been without its challenges. I, however wanted to help Josh and Jenna be successful, and I longed for the joy of that little girl that brought such delight to my heart.

In a matter of weeks, I packed all my belongings and moved to Colorado to help them. The initial weeks were exciting. I slept in Lily's room and could not have been more thrilled. She was talking like a little chatterbox. She loved dancing and clapping to the songs on the TV kid shows. It took me a few months to get a license to practice in Colorado. In the meantime, I enjoyed my days caring for Lily.

We went to the library, the science center, and the park and talked with every dog. Lily loves dogs and cats. She was always wholly enamored when one went by, no matter the animal's size. My heart still smiles at the remembrance of her spotting an animal. She was one-tracked and pounded her feet quickly toward the "puppy." When it was warm, we took in the pool on most days. It was a delightful time. But like always, fantasyland is just for a season, and then I started working.

As soon as I was hired, I decided to buy a house. We had talked and agreed that my sweet family would move in with me, and we could live and love one another the way I had always hoped. Hope abounded. The proverbial butterflies swarmed around my head, and my heart was singing.

One week after moving into the new home, the church kicked Jenna out because she questioned some things. My old wounds, not yet completely healed, opened like a festering lesion. I wrote in my journal,

> "Why did Pastor Tom make such horrible decisions? My faith in God's people to love one another is shaky! Leaders who use shotguns to shoot their sheep must stop. Where is the love? Is it hidden behind their egos? Are they so afraid of being wrong that they must shoot anyone questioning them?"

Jenna's pain brought mine up front and center, and I was angry. I cannot say I was just angry at Pastor Tom. I was angry at myself. I had just closed on the house one week prior. So, I now had a monstrous house payment, and I was unsure that Josh and Jenna would stay in Colorado.

Discontentment started almost immediately. I was frustrated that they were not cleaning up their messes to my satisfaction, and they were frustrated that I was too demanding for their satisfaction. We were all hurting. I thought of Paul in prison.

> I know what it is to be in need, and I know what it is to have plenty. I have learned the secret of being content in any and every situation, whether well-fed or hungry, whether living in plenty or want. I can do all this through him, who gives me strength (Philippians 4:12–13 NIV).

I wanted to walk in His strength and be content. With relationships in the home again encompassed in hurt, I desperately needed to cling to my Savior. I kept thinking, *Had I just taken the time to wait on God, would he have told me not to go to Colorado?* I will never know because I did not wait. I am guessing; He would have said, DON'T GO!

Lord, when will I learn? When will I stop these emotional decisions and listen? What can you do to change my compulsive behaviors? Once again, I am here in this desperate place. I know it is my fault….Again. Please help me!

All three of us were in a broken place. Life had been burdensome, and here we were in Colorado, far from friends and other family. Wounded people don't make the best decisions. So much pain was going around, and tempers were ever-present. It wasn't long before they decided to move out into a friend's townhome. This was great for them, but I was now left with a giant mortgage to pay by myself. The lost and lonely feelings deepened. I became more withdrawn. Only Lily could bring laughter to my heart. Again and again, I had run to situations to fill the loneliness of my heart only to have my heart slammed to the ground like a tsunami crushes towns. Only debris and damaged souls are left to try to rebuild. *How many more storms could I withstand and remain? When will I learn? Can I learn?*

Chapter Thirty-Five
NO PURPOSE, NO HOPE

If the enemy can isolate you, he can take you out!
—Rodney Hogue

It was only a few months before Jenna and Josh were done with their Colorado experience, and they packed up their belongings and feelings and moved back to Arkansas. With my heart still broken from the trauma that Arkansas held, combined with the third damaging church encounter and the hurt emotions of the three of us, I felt utterly paralyzed. I knew I could not return to Arkansas.

Years before, a prophet visiting our church had a word for me. "You are like the Weeble that wobbles but doesn't fall down." Funny that here in this broken place, I felt like a Weeble that wobbled, fell, and was crushed underfoot. I desperately wanted to find freedom, but my time with the Lord felt more like a check mark than something tangible and transformative. I still was not able to unlock the secret to intimacy in my relationship with Him. Even worship, which had gotten through to my heart in the worst of times, was empty.

I tried to pray, but I felt so overwhelmed with the circumstances of life that the only words I could find were ones of lament, shame, and brokenness. I became apathetic to survive. If I didn't care, I could keep going. It was as if my relationship with my Father was all but dead, and I was certain that I had killed it. I was begging God to do something or take me home. Any attempt at reading the Word felt lifeless. I had reached the bottom of all of my strength, and I could no longer do anything to help myself. Everything I read seemed to point out what a failure I was. I continued to go to church and listen to Christian radio hoping for a life-giving miracle.

The next few months were routine. I worked most days, and with the amount of driving I had to do to get to each clinic, the days were very long. I would often leave by 6 a.m. and return home at 8:30 p.m. I showered, collapsed in bed, and returned to a different clinic the next day. But the best part of each day was the majestic splendor of the mountains I traveled through during sunrise. Looking at the sun glistening on the mountain's peaks lifted my soul as if I could feel God's presence just by looking at His creation. Almost magically, a fragment of hope would spring forth like a tiny weak plant in the morning dew. Alive with the promise of possibility. my sidetracked life didn't seem to have a terminal prognosis.

Once I was back home, I was on the eternal cycle of being alone. I would love to tell you that I spent hours with the Lord and read His Word looking for the answers, but the truth is I was tired and miserable and all I could think about was escape. My one reprieve was that I found a charming used bookstore with a café in it. I would spend my off days there, where I felt relaxed and filled even though I was alone. I read copious amounts of murder mysteries, sipping coffee as if I had the best life of all.

I debated about staying in Colorado since I had just bought a house. Between losing money on the home in Arkansas, two months of not being employed, and then purchasing this house in Colorado, my finances were a bit of a disaster. I went to church by myself. I went out to eat by myself. I shopped by myself. I worked in a clinic by myself. I think you see the thread. Aside from a couple across the street and another couple beside me, I didn't interact with people unless they were seeing me at the clinic for an illness. About the only other interactions I had were with my two neighbors. They were so helpful in shoveling snow off my driveway every time it snowed. And that was worth a lot. It snowed nearly every week from October to May.

One day, a storm raged outside, matching the tempest inside me. I wanted to die! Mind you, I did not consider killing myself, but I was sincerely okay with God taking me. Laying on my couch, I remember telling God "I suck at making a difference in my own life, let alone in the Kingdom of God. Please do us both a favor, if I am never coming out of this to do something meaningful with my life, please don't keep me here. Please!"

In retrospect, I see that shame, fear and guilt had tied my soul to the past and I could not see my way out. I could barely go a year without doing some idiotic thing, all in the name of helping someone, only to bring further destruction to my life. *How could I ever make a difference in His Kingdom? Lord, if you hear me, help.* As I was lying under the skylight in my ceiling, watching the black clouds above, Nancy called. I didn't recognize it then, but God was answering my plea even as I laid waiting, partially hoping for a large hail stone to crash through the skylight and kill me.

God always knew when I needed the words of a faithful friend. I told her what I was doing. She prayed for me as I had nothing left to pray. She asked what my plans were as far as staying in Colorado. I didn't have plans. Survival was about all I could muster then, and that was not going well.

Nancy begged me to move to Tennessee and stay with her and Gary. She knew I needed healing, and she was worried about me. I didn't want to think about moving. I had moved so much already, and almost all the moves were done primarily by me. I was tired and just wanted something to go right. *What is wrong with me that I get lambasted even by those I love? Am I the heinous person some have called me out to be?* As I sobbed under the heavy cloud of hopelessness, there was no point anymore; Nancy just started to pray. Listening to her pray, I stared at the sky through the skylight, and a slight parting of the darkness began outside with a slower response inside of me. I knew I needed to change somewhere inside, or the isolation would consume me.

When Nancy was done trying to talk some sense into me, I hung up the phone with a renewed perspective and got off the couch. I put on worship music, marched around my home, and declared the words of God's truth that I desperately wanted to believe. I am sure I looked like a children's church leader as I marched around shouting the following declarations with hand motions and fisted arms to proclaim and declare victory.

> You love me even when I am unlovely. You called me by name before I was formed in my mother's womb. You have good plans for my life. You will not leave me. You are faithful even when I am unfaithful. I am the righteousness of God through Christ. You are the Good Shepherd, and You will provide and protect me. I will look to You and You will deliver me because You are faithful, and Your lovingkindness is everlasting. Let it be so in Jesus' Name!

I sang worship songs with reviving hope. By the end of the day, I sat and stared at the sky that had cleared and praised my Abba Father for my mind that had also cleared. I thanked Him for his kindness in giving me such a loving friend in Nancy.

A song by For King and Country called "Shoulders," which is based on Psalm 121:2, says, "My help comes from You Lord" played on repeat in my heart and head during that season of my life. I listened as they sang my prayer and helped me connect with my God amid my struggles. Fear of failure hovered over me as my heart was stirring. I knew I was locked in a battle.

Author Neale Walsh says, "FEAR is an acronym for False Evidence Appearing Real." But is it false evidence when my life takes another disastrous turn with every plan? I asked God, saying to Him out loud again and again: "Lord, help me know what You want me to do."

I went to church on Wednesday evening, and again I sat alone, and nobody in my large church spoke to me. I drove home in silence. The loneliness was consuming me, and I needed to get help. I knew I was prideful about being self-sufficient, and perhaps that was the very thing that God was trying to kill out of me. I could have managed where I was on my own, but would I experience any life? That was the question. As I sat quietly, I admitted my need. *What a mess I am! I am the one who generally thinks she has the answers, and here I sit again with my life in an ash heap.* Perhaps I really did need someone to lower me through the roof to the Healer, like the faithful friends in Mark 2. Nancy was that faithful friend. Instead of focusing on helping others, maybe it was time I surrendered my confounding need to remain independent and embrace the idea that I needed help and make the move to a place where I could get whole. Admittedly, I was terrified of making another move that could potentially make my life worse than it was, and while I hoped I could pray and believe that I could hear God, I could not. As I sat staring at another storm that so accurately reflected my life, I sensed darkness would swallow me if I stayed. I had to do something—even if it proved to be wrong.

I was reminded of a conversation I had with Apostle Floyd Baker, an apostle that was in leadership of the network over our church, years before when James and I were trying to hear God about doing chemotherapy. He asked me, "Donna, how big is your God? If you believe He is saying to do chemo and you are wrong, is He bigger than that?"

I said, "Yes."

He said, "If you believe He is saying, don't do chemo, and you are wrong, is He bigger than that?"

I said, "Yes."

He said, "God looks on your heart and honors your yes. Do what you believe He is saying and then don't look back. He has you." It was such simple advice that took so much pressure off our shoulders. Since I was remembering it again, about eighteen years later, it felt like it had to be God.

Going with that advice and only half believing I would hear an answer, I asked God what I should do to move forward. Suddenly, I saw the immediate changes I needed to make to the house to sell it. Seeing that changes could be made without spending a ton of money,

I believed that was my answer. The decision was made. I was moving…again!

The following weeks brought many quick changes. Selling my house only eight months after buying it and moving to Dickson, Tennessee, I knew I could lose money, but I also knew that being so far from any family or friends, I was losing myself. The war was raging, and I was being defeated. I had to be honest about that.

Preparations began. I started to pack all nonessentials in boxes to put in the garage. I made modest improvements to the home with some staging I had learned from the countless hours of HGTV. I contacted my realtor, who sold the house to me originally, and she was understanding but not overly optimistic about me walking away with any money. I trusted the voice I kept hearing in my heart and moved forward. On July 4, 2016, my house went on the market. On July 5, 2016, I had an offer that would give back the money I put down. On Aug 7, I moved out of that home with enough money to pay the movers and settle in Tennessee. Even now, this brings tears to my eyes. God is so faithful. Once again, my Abba Father came to my rescue. His goodness is truly unfailing, even when I constantly feel I am failing Him.

During my last week of work in Colorado, I stayed with the pastor's family from my church. My belongings were already in transport to Tennessee. I was excited and scared. I was excited to move to where my best friend lived but scared because I felt so broken; I didn't want to unleash my baggage on the people I loved. Nancy assured me they were ready. My last day in Colorado arrived, and I drove to the Denver airport to pick up Nancy, so we could take a road trip adventure before starting my new life in Tennessee.

Though I was still worried about taking my baggage into Nancy and Gary's life, I knew I needed a lifeline. A place I could rest and recover—a place to be cared for instead of always being the caregiver. I needed to allow them to help me and trust their acts of kindness would grow new roots of love and connection. Already with this decision, hope for a renewed life, coming forth like a sliver of light that pierces the darkness, was awakening.

Chapter Thirty-Six
NEW ROOTS

Let your roots grow down into him,
and let your lives be built on him.
—Colossians 2:7 NLT

The drive from Colorado to Tennessee with Nancy was filled with quality friend time. We visited the Grand Tetons, Yellowstone National Park, Little Big Horn, the Badlands, Mount Rushmore, and the Saint Louis Arch as we made our way to Tennessee in the warm and inviting August of 2016. My shame of not being successful remained quiet as we explored our great country's beautiful parks and history.

The adventures brought much laughter and an incredible amount of silliness, which reminded me of times past when I was not so serious. One of these times was when we first arrived in Jackson Hole, Wyoming. We stopped at a tiny country store as some hikers came into the store and offered me their bear spray that they hadn't had to use. I have no idea what prompted me to accept this gift, but I suppose it was the fact that I had never heard of bear spray, and I was very curious. Already beginning to chuckle that I held in my hand Pepper Power Magnum Bear Spray to stop an angry bear at ranges up to thirty feet, I went to show Nancy. While trying to hold in the flabbergasted giggle, I read the instructions out loud. We both erupted in a joyous belly laugh. The idea that we would ever be less than thirty feet from a bear to use the spray seemed preposterous. As I had planned the entire trip, Nancy asked "Where are we going to be that a bear can get within thirty feet of us?" I told her I didn't know, but the hikers said we might need it. Still laughing, Nancy said, "I'll run, and you spray the bear!"

No way, I laughed, "I'll run, and you spray the bear…your aim is better."

Trying to win the argument that had no point, Nancy said, "They gave you the bear spray, so you get to spray the bear."

Gleefully, we joked about bear spray and checked out. I asked the man in the store, "Do people see a lot of bears around here?"

He responded, already grinning at what may have seemed like a dumb question, "Typically, they are around campgrounds and on the trails where they might find food."

After a little more discussion, we determined that we were extremely unlikely to make use of this gift. Another string of jokes and the man behind the counter was now in good humor and joking back with us. We finished our purchases and made our way to the parking lot. Out in the parking lot, we suddenly came upon a six-foot angry bear!

Facing the bear eye-to-eye, quickly, I grabbed the canister, turned it toward the bear, growled my scariest growl and gave my fiercest mean face and sprayed the bear. Nancy, already taking pictures of the mountains surrounding us, quickly turned and snapped a picture of me facing the angry bear. The bear was completely unaffected and just stood there very still. It might have been because the bear was a statue at the entrance to the store. Another outburst of jokes and then the hilarity took a pause as we turned and found real backpackers and gave them the bear spray. They were grateful and we wished them well. The silliness was palpable to my soul, and it felt so good to experience.

Revelation hit me. I had not laughed out loud, from my gut, unrestrained in nearly two years. Laughter was indeed much needed medicine I had been missing. My dear friend came to bring me to her home, and already she was lightening the load of my heavy heart with the many opportunities to be like children and laugh ourselves to tears.

This time was a gift away from the dark and desperate place I had been living and a small glimmer of hope was born.

When I arrived in Tennessee, Nancy and her husband, Gary, embraced me in every way. I felt more peace than I had experienced for so long. Nancy and Gary represented Jesus well to me. Coming to their home was the beginning of my healing journey. There was still much work ahead to find my way, but I felt loved and cared for and I was in a safe space to heal. This environment brought a softening in the soil of my heart, which would allow for healthy new roots to grow.

I was broken but not beyond redemption. I met with my Savior on the front porch of their cabin in the woods. I began to hear His voice again. I was emotional, vulnerable, and desperate to receive His help through it all. I was beyond trying to fix myself. I had hit the bottom of my own strength. I was ready to wave the white flag of surrender to Him and to REALLY let Him have my life. Surrender started for me from a recognition that I may go astray and destroy my life apart from my Father. He is my inheritance. Any decision that doesn't involve Him is likely to end up in chaos. I had been in a spiritual wilderness and floundering through life at times for many years.

There are many lessons I have learned in the past years; each is powerful and life changing. One of the greatest revelations in my life came about five-and-a-half years after coming to Tennessee. God revealed my entire life has been shaped by shame. It didn't start when Judy died in my car wreck, which I had assumed. Rather, it was attached to me in the womb. I know that may seem an odd thing to say…but let me explain.

Each of my parents were raised during the Great Depression, and neither of them was wanted by their parents. This fact was something they always knew and carried—even as adults. Their stories were not so unlike mine. In the fact that they ran from pain in their homes, trying to grasp a life free of agony, only to make decisions leading to greater hurt—just like I had done.

My dad lied about his age to get into the Marine Corps at age sixteen to get away from his home. My mom married my immature father when he was nineteen and she was eighteen to get out of her home. Dad never saw himself as a loved son, and Mom never saw herself as a loved daughter. Committed to marriage, they did their best to raise a family. But two broken people will go on to produce after their kind if they never receive healing. All three of their children have also struggled with shame as part of their identities on some level.

For me, shame was a consistent theme. When I didn't feel good about myself, I had to protect myself from others. I did this by trying to remain in control of every situation so others could not see the real me. I guess you could say that I made myself into my own God. If I was hiding, then I was protecting myself because I feared others' opinions of me. If I was protecting myself, it was because my love relationship with God was failing. I was beginning to see a richer truth. There is no shame in love. Psalm 34:4–5 NIV says, "I sought the Lord, and he answered me, he delivered me from all my fears. Those who look to him are radiant, their faces are never covered with shame." This verse begs the question: *Why was I struggling with letting others see the real me? Why was I hiding?* The answer can only be, there was a breach in my love relationship with Christ and I had not yet tapped into the wholeness found in that love relationship. It is essential to know and to believe I can trust Him to protect me.

Not too long after I began to understand the effects of shame on my life, God spoke to me one day that I also had an orphan spirit. When I first heard this term, I assumed this spirit attached itself to me when my mom and husband had died within the same week. I actually agreed with this spirit when I said to the people in my family, "I became an orphan and a widow in the same week." But, later, God showed me that the orphan spirit also came in the womb, because that is the reflection of a soul when it doesn't know who they are or whose they are. For so much of my life, I was resistant to getting close to others…because I thought they would reject me when I was no longer of value to them. I became strong in my own strength so that I would not need others. That is what my Abba was teaching me. Orphans have no home, nobody to trust, no one they know they can count on. I felt unseen my entire life, which translated to me as unloved. Because I didn't feel loved, that meant that I had no value.

Each victory only made me feel good until the next perceived failure, and when I failed, then a previous victory had no power or meaning in my life. The intimacy I was seeking could never be experienced until the Father healed the little girl in me. I began to see that His love is the key to transformation, so I cried out for the Love of God to transform me. As I have drawn closer to Him, the little girl in me has learned to stand on Papa's shoes and let Him lead me.

Psalm 139 is filled with gold about how God sees me, and I find myself meditating on it to find redemption in His love. I rejoice when I read the following words "How precious are your thoughts about me, O God. They cannot be numbered! I can't even count them; they outnumber the grains of the sand! And when I wake up, you are still with me!" (Psalm 139, 17–18). Surrendering to Him leaves me in great hands, and I will trust and surrender to that kind of LOVE for the rest of my life!

I certainly have not arrived, and I will not be complete until I am face to face with Him. But I am healing and growing into the things He has for me. His gift of love offers hope in my hopelessness, strength in my weakness, joy in my brokenness, and all I have to do is look up and say, "PAPA, ABBA, come meet me here." All He requires of me is my FULL SURRENDER!

ACKNOWLEDGMENTS

So many people have encouraged me and loved me through what sometimes was a grueling process in life. The list would be endless with those who have fluttered by and left grace where they touched me, but I must honor one incredible woman who has been a strong tower when I could not find the strength to pray. Nancy Carter is as faithful a friend as a person could ever wish for. Despite leaving much of our story out of these pages, this story has her fingerprints all over it, and it likely would not have existed had it not been for the love and patience that Nancy has given to me. Bless you, Nancy. I will never be the same because you walked into my life. God saw the necessity to grace me with such a woman.

Though from a completely different place and time, I must give grand honor to Missy Maxwell-Worton, my writing coach. Apart from her teaching and wisdom, this book would not be before you now. Apart from her prayers and encouragement, it would likely be written from a less healed place. I also want to honor the Warrior Writers Group. This group of ladies, led by Missy, have helped me come to a place of healing to produce this work. The faithfulness of this group to listen, pray, and speak to the broken places has been one of the most extraordinary healing experiences I have ever had the pleasure of being a part of.

Thank you to each of you for the part you played in helping me face and defeat the giants that sought to keep my destiny from me. Shame and fear were two of the biggest giants, but several other equal-opportunity offenders also existed. Then there is the giant of my mind. "I can't" and "I am not good enough" tried to rob me of precious jewels. Gosh, I love each of you intensely. Thank you so much for your continued love and support. I shall always be grateful.

One more thing. Though Mrs. Peggy Butler and Norma Grey are already in Heaven, I would like to offer thanks to my loving Father for gracing my life with these two beautiful women. Though my life has been a bit of a roller coaster, the foundation that they both helped build ensured I didn't walk away from God in my most broken times. Their memories live on in my heart and now in this book. I love you both and look forward to meeting you again in Heaven.

APPENDIX

This list contains books and materials that have ministered to me, shaped me, and healed me. I don't have quotes from any of these books because I was trying to stick with my authentic voice. However, their fingerprints are represented in this work.

Books

Leif Hetland, *Healing the Orphan Spirit*

Rodney Hogue, *Forgiveness*

Andrew Murray, *Absolute Surrender*

A.W. Tozer, *No Greater Love: Experiencing The Heart of Jesus*

Recommended Prayers

Lynn Eldridge, "Prayer to Renounce Suicidal Thoughts," https://www.lynneldridge.com/prayer

A Life-changing Resource
For steps to beginning a relationship and finding peace with God, see Billy Graham's excellent explanation at https://stepstopeace.org/

NOTES

1. "Quote by Bryant McGill," *Best Positive Quotes*, accessed 12/7/2023, https://www.bestpositivequotes.com/author/bryant-mcgill/whatever-makes-you-uncomfortable-is-your-biggest-opportunity-for-growth.

2. "Lessons On Forgiveness from T.D. Jakes," *NPR: Special Series—Wisdom Watch*, Heard on *Tell Me More*, April 5, 2012, accessed October 26,2023.

3. "Henry Cloud Quotes," Goodreads, accessed 10/18/2024, https://www.goodreads.com/author/quotes/1114699.Henry_Cloud

4. The Dysfunctional Family," *Institute of Counseling*, July 14, 2020, accessed 12/7/2023, https://instituteofcounseling.org/the-dysfunctional-family/.

5. "Denis Diderot Quotes," *BrainyQuote*, accessed 12/7/2023, https://www.brainyquote.com/quotes/denis_diderot_108338.

6. "Think About What You Are Thinking About," June 6, 2024, Joyce Meyer Ministries, accessed 10/18/2024, https://joycemeyer.org/DailyDevo/2024/06/06-Think-About-What-You-Are-Thinking-About.

www.ingramcontent.com/pod-product-compliance
Lightning Source LLC
Chambersburg PA
CBHW070917120626
46546CB00001B/299